Laughing All the Way to Work

A SURVIVAL GUIDE FOR TODAY'S ADMINISTRATIVE ASSISTANT

PATRICIA ROBB

with Lynn Crosbie & Krysta Anstey

PORTLAND • OREGON
INKWATERPRESS.COM

Disclaimer: The opinions expressed in this book are those of the author. Nothing in this book should be considered legal advice, but rather the author's own experience, tips and hints.

I am not responsible for the content on any sites I have referenced as a resource in this book. These independent sites are subject to change by their site operators and I have no control over the content.

www.inkwaterpress.com

ISBN-10 1-59299-354-0
ISBN-13 978-1-59299-354-3

Publisher: Inkwater Press

Printed in the U.S.A.
All paper is acid free and meets all ANSI standards for archival quality paper.

*Dedicated to Michelle Lavictoire who first gave me
the idea of writing this book*

Foreword

Whether you prefer the term *assistant* or are comfortable with *secretary*, this is a treasure trove of wit and wisdom for the person behind the successful executive or professional. From the interview that wins you the job to becoming the executive or professional's indispensable right arm, Patricia has mined her years of experience and insightful observation to put together this fun and fundamental how-to guide.

Patricia provides invaluable insights into the tricks of the trade. She provides simple but common-sense advice on how to conduct yourself from the first impressions at the job interview to learning the ropes and becoming the *go-to* person among your peers. From the minutiae of grammar and typographical errors to the big picture of "Do You Have a Job or a Career?" she shares her down-to-earth perspective with a sense of humour that reminds us that no job can be tackled successfully without being able to laugh at ourselves and the vagaries of the workplace.

The experienced *assistant* will enjoy her humorous outlook and perspective on the various aspects of the job and will identify with her as she explores such timely issues as cell phone etiquette ("When Using Your Cell Phone Can Be Bad Manners"), blogging ("Blogging, Social Networking and Work: Do They Mix?") and the increasing presence of women in positions of influence ("When You Go to the Bathroom With Your Boss: Same-Sex Working Relationships"). Her perspective can be comical but is always seriously directed toward getting the job done as efficiently and effectively as possible.

I daresay, this might be just the book to give to your boss. He or she would certainly benefit from this insight into the complexity and demands of the position of administrative assistant and the perceptive boss might not be so tempted to take for granted the person who prepares correspondence, makes travel arrangements and organizes their meetings and events.

Whether you cherry-pick the sections of this book that interest you most or read it from cover to cover, it is sure to amuse and enlighten you. You will be congratulating yourself on the aspects of the job you do well and will find yourself using Patricia's helpful hints to improve your performance in other areas.

You will almost certainly feel more empowered and respectful of your own professionalism.

Susan Adams
Freelance Editor

Acknowledgements

I would like to thank my family and friends and all my co-workers. In particular, my co-workers Diane, Kathi, Darlene, Sharon, Brad, Kathy, Joanne and my two bosses, Russel and Daphne, for their patience with me as they put up with all my book-writing talk.

I want to thank my network of administrative assistants without whom I would not have been able to write this book. Thank you to Denise Bellfoy, friend and Executive Assistant, for finally giving in to all my nagging and letting me interview her for The Art of Minute Taking.

Thank you to Susan Adams, freelance editor, for her encouragement and constructive criticism. It was much appreciated.

Thank you to JoAnn who offered her assistance and expertise in reviewing the interview questions and answers.

Thank you to Martha, a co-worker, who assisted me with an article, and to Anthony for laughing at my jokes and letting me use him as an example far too many times.

Thank you to all my IAAP professional friends.

Thanks to my good friend Sue and my special friend Gary who encouraged me to get into writing because they "just love reading my e-mails."

A special thanks to my sister Lynn for her insistence that I not give up and for all her help with editing, proofing and writing. A special thanks as well to my daughter Krysta for being part of this project and offering her expertise in the kitchen. She has been cooking for me since she was five years old when she first surprised me with a Mother's Day breakfast in bed of soggy toast and cereal.

And thanks to God for plunking me in the middle of the copyright section of a law firm and seating me across from a freelance editor just at the time I started to write. That was a good one.

Preface

I wanted to write a book that people would actually read and have fun with, but could also use as a reference book for good hints and tips to make their jobs easier. I also wanted to write something they could pick up on the bus and have a chuckle or two while reading on the way to work.

I have tried to make it entertaining, filled with real stories and examples, and of course some humour too. I have put time and effort into writing about my experiences and things I have learned over the years that would help anyone pursuing a career as an administrative professional.

Laughing and *Survival* are key words in the title because I feel without the one you could never do the other. We all have to work, but who says you can't enjoy it too?

In a sense we can also be seen as *Laughing All the Way to Work* when we are skilled, prepared and equipped to do our jobs.

How I got started?

I was curious what a blog was so decided to search it out. "What could I write about," I wondered? Well, I had been an administrative assistant for almost 30 years. Certainly I knew enough about that to pass on a few tips and hints. So I created a blog and started to write and I haven't stopped since.

I printed my blog articles and brought them home one evening. A friend saw it and was so impressed with the size of it she said I should write a book. I took her suggestion to heart and here is my book of blog articles. My blog can be found at http://www.secretaryhelpline.blogspot.com/.

I keep thinking I am going to run out of ideas, but every day I go into work I come home with something new that I want to share with my readers. It may be a common-sense idea I was taught or learned along the way, some mistake I made that I am still kicking myself over, some new hint I found to make my job easier or some funny incident encountered on the way to work or at work. So here it is. I hope you enjoy it and I hope it will encourage you to be the best that you can be in what you do.

What's in a name?

When I am asked what I do for a living, I usually say I am an administrative assistant. As an old-timer, however, I still sometimes use the term *secretary* when describing my job.

A friend of mine thinks that since our title change to administrative assistant our workloads have increased and she longs for the day she could be *just a secretary* again. Our role has certainly evolved into something more demanding, but in my opinion much more interesting. I enjoy the challenges of being an administrative assistant and I like the title change, but sometimes the word administrative assistant is just too formal or too stuffy for me. I guess I am old enough to be comfortable referring to myself as a *secretary* without being offended, but for the purposes of this book I will be using the terms administrative assistant and secretary interchangeably.

Table of Contents

PART III – OFFICE MANNERS   57

PART IV – TEAMBUILDING   77

PART V – MEETING PLACES   93

PART VIII – OFFICE ETIQUETTE POEMS   177

PART IX (A) - THE REST OF YOUR LIFE:
KEEPING A BALANCE   185

PART IX (B) – HELP FROM A CHEF WITH HINTS, TIPS
AND RECIPES FOR TODAY'S BUSY WORKER   195

PART I – GETTING STARTED

Chapter 1

Preparing Your Resume

I was working for a government organization when I heard news reports that the public sector was in for some big layoffs due to downsizing. The rumour mill was in full swing at work.

I was in a union environment, but I was at the bottom of the years-of-service ladder as I had only been there a year. Was there any hope I would keep my job? Things were not looking good. I got the news a few weeks later that about a dozen of us were going to be laid off, including myself.

It is a hard thing to lose your job, but it does happen and if this has happened to you, the sooner you get back on your feet the better. Fortunately for me my employer sent me on career counselling as part of the *downsizing package*. Not everyone will have this opportunity so I wanted to share with you some things I learned.

I feel that even during a seemingly bad experience, you can always learn something positive. One of the things I remember, and have put to good use, was a workshop on resume writing. I hope this will help you to write your own resume if you are looking for a job or if you just need to update your old resume.

In resume writing it is suggested that any experience over 10 years is too old to put on your resume. "What? They don't want to know about my summer job as a babysitter?"

And no need to list your duties as that is considered to be old-style resume writing. This was radical for me. I was used to listing all my duties on my resume: maintaining a filing system, answering the telephone, typing correspondence, etc. Instead they recommended setting out your skills and strengths in point form right up front so the potential employer can see if you have the skills for the job.

Under years of experience, rather than putting four years' experience try, "almost five years of progressive achievement"; or for "11 years of experience" try, "over 10 years of progressive achievement." I must admit it did sound more impressive.

I use this format in writing my resume and have always had good comments from potential employers, especially on the fact that it is so easy to read. And let's face it, we want them to read it. (See Appendix II at the back of the book for a Sample Resume).

* * * * * * * * * * * * * * * * * *

"When one door closes, another opens; but we often look so long and so regretfully upon the closed door that we do not see the one which has opened for us."
ALEXANDER GRAHAM BELL

Chapter 2

Interview Preparation

I had an interview at 11, but I was busy with my job, my father was in the hospital and I was trying to arrange an engagement party for my daughter. I just didn't have time to bring my clothes to the dry cleaner, and worse than that I had an inch of grey roots showing and hadn't coloured my hair. I finally decided that they would have to take me as I was because I didn't have the time to do everything I knew I should to prepare for this interview.

It ended up that I did get the job. They mustn't have noticed my grey roots or wrinkled suit, or I completely wowed them with my skills and humour, but this definitely was not the way to go to an interview!

Is it important what you wear to the interview?

The first thing the potential employer will see when you walk in the door is what you are wearing. It is very important to make that first impression count. I have found that a business suit is always appropriate. (See Part I - Chapter 6 - *Dressing for the Office* for more tips and suggestions).

How will you conduct yourself during the interview?

Will you be relaxed and confident during the interview or uptight and nervous? How do you get to the point where you are relaxed and confident and how do you make that good first impression?

The key is to be prepared. Go over some possible interview questions and answers. There are some very good websites that give sample questions and answers, but try to make the answers your own. Go over these questions, no matter how silly some of them seem, believe me, they do ask them! Get a friend or family member to ask you questions and practice your answers. (See Appendix II for *30 Interview Questions and Answers* and *Questions YOU can ask in the interview*).

You should research the company where you are applying. It is good to be familiar with what the company does. Most companies have a web page that will provide very helpful information.

Most importantly, read the job posting and determine if your skills match the requirements for the job and if you think you will be able to meet the challenge. If you believe you will, then you can go confidently into the interview knowing you can do the job and that will come across to the people interviewing you. If your skills fall short of what is required for this particular job posting, you may want to pass this opportunity by (at least this time around). You can always take courses to learn the required skills and upgrade your present skills for the next time.

One thing we tend to forget when we go for an interview is that the company has to sell you on the job as well. Ask questions and find out if this is the job you want. I always feel an interview has been a success when it has turned into a conversation. There should be questions from both sides of the table.

What about that all important question "What salary are you looking for?" You should have a figure in mind before you go into the interview, but it is also OK to ask "What salary are you offering?"

Anything you can do to set yourself apart from everyone else will help. Send a thank you note or card to the people who interviewed you. It <u>will</u> be noticed.

Whether you are successful or not, an interview is never a waste of time. You can always learn from the experience and see what the expectations are and what the job market is like.

Something to consider...

I read an article about interviewing and the writer said that after an interview the executive who was interviewing went to the admin assistant and asked what she thought about the candidate. Unfortunately, the candidate had been rude to the assistant and impatient while waiting.[1] Not a good move on that person's part.

Never underestimate the seemingly little people. We may look like we are just sitting behind our desk smiling and answering the phone, but if an employer is smart they recognize we can be their eyes and ears and our opinion counts.

If you want to make a good impression, be nice to the receptionist, the doorman, the janitor and the person who gets your coffee while you wait. The interview starts the minute you walk in the building.

* * * * * * * * * * * * * * * * * * * *

Quitting a job before finding out for sure you have another one is like getting on an elevator with a full bladder. You hope you don't get stuck.

---

1 Bruzzese, Anita, 45 Things, *Impress the Hiring Manager -- and the Receptionist*, http://www.45things.com/blog.php (accessed March 9, 2008)

TIME OUT

Job posting with a *twist*

After reading numerous job postings for administrative assistants (most re-quiring candidates to walk on water), I thought I would write this job posting from an assistant's point of view.

Administrative assistant seeks professional for a great working oppor-tunity. Applicants must be respectful of their assistant and have a good understanding of everything they do in a day. The professional should be willing to work with the assistant on projects and give as much detail as possible to complete the task. The ideal candidate must have excellent management and communication skills and a professional demeanour.

The administrative assistant is seeking someone who will not hover, but will leave the urgent task with clear instructions on when it is needed and what is required, and then return to their office to work on other matters. Applicants must write clearly and if using short forms, explain what they mean.

The applicant must be someone who is mindful of the time it takes to do tasks when passing on many projects. The applicant must never be demeaning or roll their eyes.

Aptitude tests will be given in Outlook Calendar to ensure proper scheduling techniques and in Word to avoid formatting problems when passing work onto the assistant.

Chapter 3

The Dreaded Probationary Period

fter eight years in one position I decided to look for another job. I sent out my resume, secured an interview and eventually was offered the job. During my negotiations we discussed salary and benefits and my start date, but it never occurred to me that I would need to go through a probationary period.

Once I gave my notice at the other place of employment and started my new job it hit me with full force, "I was on probation for three months."

It scared me and made me feel vulnerable and I wondered if I had made a mistake making the move. I was already in a secure position, why did I leave it to go to this uncertainty?

I worked hard in those three months. I felt I needed to prove myself all over again, but every night I went home wondering if I had. It wasn't until my three-month anniversary when I was filling out my self evaluation on my performance appraisal that one of my new bosses came by and asked what I was doing. When I told him what I was filling out he said, "Oh that should be easy, you are doing a great job!" I was never so relieved and thankful to hear those words. I just regretted that someone had not said something to me earlier about my performance and I wish that psychologically I had prepared myself for this time of probation. It would have saved me a lot of anxious days and nights while I adjusted to my new position.

I have learned a few things since those days and would like to pass them on so you can be better prepared for this time of learning and fitting into your new job.

Early in my probation I was speaking to some co-workers about this and I found out that the length of the probation period can be negotiable. I had thought of everything else in my negotiations, but had neglected this important one.

Shortly after this experience a friend of mine was in the same position. She was offered a job and was considering the move, but the probationary period of six months was holding her back from making the decision. Other than the length of the probation, the job opportunity and career possibilities were excellent. She negotiated with them and was able to decrease the time to three months.

An employer needs to have a probationary period in case the fit is not right, but the length of the probation is usually negotiable.

I also discovered that the probationary period is an excellent time to ask questions and learn. Never be afraid to ask questions, especially during this stage in your career. Some people think it might reflect badly on them, but when I have worked with new employees I always appreciate hearing their questions. It helps me gauge how much they are taking in and it gives me confidence that they are on the right track and lets me know if I need to give further teaching and coaching. Your new employer expects there will be a learning curve. Take advantage of this time and ask questions.

I would also recommend that you introduce yourself to your new co-workers and appreciate them for their expertise and experience. You will find they can be your greatest resource. In most cases they will want to help you to get up to speed as quickly as you can because it is in their best interests to have you able to take on your full duties and become part of the team and in some cases relieve their workloads.

The probationary period may be necessary, but it doesn't have to be scary.

Chapter 4

The Performance Appraisal: How Are You Performing?

I don't look forward to filling out my performance appraisal form, especially the self evaluation. My mind seems to go completely blank when it comes to listing my achievements and what goals I want to accomplish. It reminds me of when I went to a doctor's appointment while I was pregnant. As soon as the doctor asked me if I had any questions, I couldn't think of a thing to ask. All the books I had read recommended that you write your questions down and bring them with you. Simple, but effective and it can work the same way when you are preparing for your performance appraisal. You can start by keeping a record of complimentary e-mails you have received and successes you are particularly proud of. I received a nice e-mail from a client recently and thought that this e-mail was something that I should keep for appraisal time.

I have created a subfolder in Outlook called *Performance Appraisal* and this is where I put these types of e-mails. For instance, if I arranged a successful conference or if I was involved in a project that I am proud of, I send myself a short message detailing that, which I then drag and drop into my *Performance Appraisal* subfolder. When it comes time for my next review I read over the e-mails and am better equipped to fill out a more thorough and well thought out appraisal form.

Don't let it sneak up on you

Another way to prepare for your performance review is to get a copy of the appraisal form ahead of time so you can start thinking about the questions and write down notes that will prompt you come appraisal time. You should be able to get this from your Human Resources Department.

Each of our appraisal forms will be different, but there are some common questions that are asked and I have listed some of them to get you thinking.

What are your key accomplishments?

This is where the collection of notes and e-mails will come in handy to remind you about your accomplishments. We do so much throughout the year it is easy to forget about some of the older accomplishments.

What are your goals?

Do you have goals that you have set for yourself in your position? If not, think of some things that are doable. Maybe your goals are related to your supervisor's goals, in which case you would need to brush up on what those goals are and how your goals can relate.

Evaluate yourself

Many performance appraisal forms have an evaluation form that is ranked by the employee and their supervisor. If you rank yourself high, be prepared to explain why.

Some things to think about are:

- What is the quality of your work?
- What is the quantity of work and how are you handling it?
- How is your time management? Are you reliable and do you have a good attendance record?
- Are you able to adapt to change?
- Do you take responsibility for your work or do you play the *blame game?*
- How is your written and oral communication?
- Are you a team player? Do you get along with your co-workers?
- Do you show leadership skills?
- Do you demonstrate the required skills for the job?

+ How are your problem-solving and decision-making skills?
+ How are your planning and organization skills?
+ Are you able to delegate?
+ Do you comply with company policies?
+ Are you self motivated? Are you able to motivate others?

Personal development

These are the steps you are taking to further your career. This includes courses and training programs and would also be a good place to put your involvement in your professional organization. (See Part II – Chapter 2 *Joining a Professional Association: Is it Beneficial?*)

Some other things to consider would be:

+ Is there any training that you believe is necessary to fulfill the requirements of your position?
+ What steps are you considering to further your development? This could be on your own initiative and personal time or on-the-job training opportunities.

The performance appraisal is important

Don't downplay the Performance Appraisal. In some organizations raises are tied to how well you do. It is also a record that is kept on your personnel file and you want it to reflect accurately how you are performing. Don't be afraid to ask questions and get clarification if you need it.

Performance Appraisal Meetings are also a time for your boss to let you know about any upcoming jobs they may want you to be involved in. You need to ensure they know what your workload is like now. Something may need to be taken away before you can take on more work and this is the time to discuss it. Taking on new jobs can be rewarding, so don't miss the opportunity to learn something new to keep your job interesting and challenging.

TIME OUT

The Little Things

Holding an elevator door
Catching the bus on time
A smile
A helping hand
A pat on the back
My raise!

Chapter 5

Do You Have a Job or a Career?

A career can be defined as "the job or series of jobs that you do during your working life, especially if you continue to get better jobs and earn more money...." A *job* can be defined as "...the regular work which a person does to earn money."[2]

Here are some questions you can ask yourself to determine whether you have a job or a career.

Do you decide on a job because of availability and salary or because it is a wise career choice?

Hopefully the salary and wise career choice will go together, but you want to weigh the advantages and disadvantages to your career before you jump into a job. Some jobs may appeal to you because of the salary, but are not the best career choice. Think about your career goals when applying for a job. Will this job get you where you want to be?

Let's face it, we all need money, but is our whole purpose just to get a pay cheque and go home at the end of the day or is our goal to earn the best salary possible while advancing in our career?

Is your job challenging?

Are you looking for ways you can improve your performance? Are you looking for innovative ideas on how you can fulfill your role? Are you open

---

2 Cambridge Dictionaries Online, Cambridge Advanced Learner's Dictionary, http://dictionary.cambridge.org/ (accessed February 22, 2008)

to making changes? The answers to these questions can help you evaluate your current position and performance and determine what you can do to make it more interesting and challenging.

Are you investing in your career?

Do you upgrade your skills? Do you read books on topics of interest to your career? Do you subscribe to useful feeds and e-bulletins? We can all use extra courses or workshops to give us the edge and to keep us up to date in our field.

Do you consider yourself a professional?

Our bosses are professionals in their field. One of the certainties is they will join their professional association for their particular area. It is just a smart career choice.

Administrative assistants have professional associations. Do you know about them? Can they benefit you? Can you benefit them? Our professional associations recognize that we are experts in our field and they want to hear from us. How do we see ourselves?

If you are interested in a career, consider becoming a member of your professional association. Invest time to further your career and network with others in your field of work.

Do you believe that what you do is important and is making a difference to your organization?

You are an important part of the team and your skills are needed to effectively complete a project or job. Many organizations recognize this and show their appreciation by including you in their successes by thanking you and acknowledging your contribution. But whether your organization does so or not, it is how you view your role that is important to your career.

You will need to decide for yourself if you have a job or a career and once you do you need to determine "Is this what I want?"

Chapter 6
Dressing for the Office

Many years ago something happened that brought home to me the importance of what we wear to the office, and that some people just don't know what is appropriate office wear.

I was making my way to the photocopier and was intent on getting there, when I rounded the corner and there she was in the most ridiculous outfit I had ever seen. In surprise, the first thing that popped out of my mouth was -- "Nice outfit!" My next thought was, "Oh no, now I've encouraged her to wear it again." But the damage had been done, I couldn't take it back.

Do we need articles on what to wear to the office? Unfortunately, I think we do.

At a few places I worked they arranged for a fashion consultant to come in to specifically talk about dressing for the office. It was an excellent idea, but it made me even more aware of how important it is to the employer how we represent ourselves at work by the clothing that we wear.

"What am I going to wear?" has often been the cry in my household and I'm sure in many others as we get up in the morning and look in our closets and nothing seems suitable to wear that day. We want to look good and sometimes we need help.

Fashion consultants can do exactly that for you. They will go shopping with you and pick out business outfits and then help you choose things to go with them. The fashion consultant can help you get stylish, but not all of us have the money to hire one.

The consultant who came to my office did however give us some very practical ideas. Their first tip I had already learned many years before and knew that this was good advice: invest in a few good quality suits. The initial cost is high, but it will be worth it because they will last you for many years. Some classic styles just stand the test of time and in order to update the suit all you need to do is buy some blouses and scarves to accessorize it to bring it up to date.

Before you start to say you can't afford it, let me explain. If you think about it you will notice that when you go to the cheaper discount department stores and buy a poorer quality suit, you will be back to buy another one sooner because in most cases it will not last and will lose its shape and style. I think if you added up what you spend on clothing in a year by going back and forth to these department stores you would be very surprised at how much money it has ended up costing you. Buying good clothing is an investment in yourself and your career.

For office wear I would suggest you take a more conservative approach and you will never go wrong. I recommend you do not wear low-cut tops, skirts that are too short or pants that are too tight.

For men a business suit is very office appropriate. I have noticed that men have a greater selection in the colours of shirts they can choose from that look really nice. I have seen some men with soft yellows, nice blues and greens, startling whites and even pink shirts that have been very becoming and not too loud. The choice of tie is also important and should be colour coordinated to the shirt. There is a men's shop in the building next to mine where most of the shirts are sold along with the matching tie, making it very easy for those who do not feel that fashion is their area of expertise. If you need assistance however, the sales people are very helpful and knowledgeable. A good tip would be to make sure your socks match the colour of your suit.

For suggestions on some good hairstyle choices for men and women in the office see Part I, Chapter 7, *Are you Having a Good Office Hair Day?*

Casual days

If your office has casual days, that does not mean frayed and grungy jeans, but rather you should wear a good pair of jeans or pants and a nice shirt or top.

In the summer, never wear shorts or halter dresses, but wear a nice pair of jeans or capris with a cotton shirt, or a dress or skirt. The same goes for the men, no shorts in the office.

A good idea would be to have a suit jacket or a sweater handy at your desk because of the air conditioning.

Personal hygiene

I would not recommend wearing a fragrance to work as it can make the workplace unbearable for those who are allergic. A good deodorant should be used and teeth should be brushed. I would recommend you also use a mouthwash.

Personal hygiene is something that may not be talked about, but that doesn't mean people aren't aware of it.

Smell and tell

A woman I worked with told me that someone had mentioned to her that she had body odour. I was a young woman at the time and unfortunately didn't know how to reply. Instead of telling her the truth, I hemmed and hawed and finally said, "What an awful thing that was for someone to say to you." I then proceeded to recommend some good deodorants and showering and laundering habits. I didn't say yes, but my round-about answer was saying yes.

The person who had told her the truth initially had actually done the proper thing and did her a favour by telling her.

It is a difficult thing to talk to people about such personal issues. I think that generally it would be the HR Manager's responsibility to approach employees about such sensitive topics, but if you have a friend who has this problem, it would be a good-friend thing to tell them in a kind and gentle way.

I have since completely lost the sense of smell so if someone asked me this type of question now, I could honestly say, "I have no idea." Although now I often have to wonder, how do *I* smell and would anyone tell me if I had body odour? Hmm! Something to think about as I shower and put on my deodorant in the morning!

TIME OUT

What is that smell?

I was losing my ability to smell, but didn't realize how bad it had gotten until one day while driving with my daughter. "I smell stew," I told my daughter. She quickly turned to me and said, "Mom it's not stew." "There's a dead skunk on the road."

Chapter 7

Are you Having a Good Office Hair Day?

A trip to the hairdresser and your hair is perfect. It has bounce and shine and feels wonderful. But will you repeat it on Monday morning when you are getting ready to go into the office? Does your hairstyle matter in the workplace and, if so, what is it saying about you to your employer?

80's stare is yesterday's hair

It may have looked good in the 80s, but, newsflash, big hair is out. If you are still sporting it, "I don't like change" could be the message that is getting across loud and clear.

Your hairdresser is a good resource to ask what would look best on you in terms of colour and style. Inform your hairdresser that you are an office professional and together you can take a few moments to look at some hairstyle books and magazines for up-to-date styles. Be realistic and open to suggestions if you tend to be the type who digs your heels in and says, "Don't do anything different."

Punk rockers

The 70's spiky hairdo with lots of product may say, "I don't want anyone telling me what to do." In an office environment that promotes a team attitude, you could be giving the impression of not wanting to fit in.

Some suggestions are popular styles with lots of movement such as mid-length bobs, shags and straight cuts with shape and interesting lines.

These are very adaptable hairstyles and can have style and be practical for the office. Add some rollers for a bouncy look or straighten it for a sleek, neat style. Flattering colour and highlights can add a very professional and stylish look to your office image.

Your hairdresser will take into consideration your hair type, skin tone, facial shape and lifestyle when suggesting styles. Customers often come into a hair salon with very fine straight hair, but show their hairdresser a picture of a model with thick voluminous hair with lots of body and announce, "I want my hair to look like that." Well, you might want it, but it is not going to happen. When you are looking through the books let your hairdresser help direct you to styles that will actually work with your hair type.

The long and short of it

A long hairstyle, if it is without style, can appear plain and reminiscent of the 60s. It might be giving the impression of someone who lacks new and creative ideas. Long hair can be made more stylish by putting in some colour and long layers, while adding bounce and movement to your hair.

Straightening your long layers will give your hair a very flattering and current look that would look good in the office or at a conference while taking registration and greeting clients.

Another simple and practical long hairstyle that is suitable for the office is the ponytail. Wearing a ponytail lower on your neck with a nice clip can look very stylish. If you wear your ponytail tight and high it tends to look too sporty for a business look.

Short, severe haircuts may suggest someone who is all business with no personality. "Will you be a good addition to the company?" is what they might be thinking.

Short hair doesn't have to be boring. Ask your hairdresser to add flattering lines and textures to the cut to bring it up to date. Adding highlights on short hair can be fun and creative, while still maintaining a professional look.

What about men?

The role of the administrative assistant is mainly dominated by women, but there are men among us. The male administrative assistant should look professional and well groomed too.

A short man's haircut should be kept trimmed with regular monthly trips to the barber. Good styling products can add style and create an up to date and professional look. Your hairdresser will be able to help you make the best selection for your hair type and the style you want to achieve.

A male assistant who prefers longer hair can appear professional in a conservative men's ponytail while still maintaining his individuality.

Mirror, mirror on the wall

Take a look in the mirror and ask yourself, "What is my look saying to a potential employer or to my current employer?" Taking the time to update your style can go a long way in presenting yourself as a professional in your office.

* *

TIME OUT

It's not always black and white

I am dark haired and was looking for something to hide the hair on my upper lip. I thought I had found the answer when I discovered facial bleach. It was great. There was no pain and the hair on my upper lip seemed to disappear.

One day when I was helping at a children's club at my Church I noticed a six-year old boy looking over at me. I could tell he wanted to ask me something and finally he blurted out, "Do men have black moustaches and women have white?"

Chapter 8

When you Open the Cereal Box Upside Down: Getting Ready for Work on Time

*I*t is inevitable that on the morning I oversleep and the radio is announcing traffic is backed up and it will be slow-going to work, that is the morning I open the cereal box upside down sending my cat scrambling and leaving me with a shower of raisins and flakes at my feet.

Mornings can be a busy time. Ideally, I would like to have lots of time to make my lunch, do my hair, put on my make-up and get dressed, but most mornings I find myself racing just to get out the door.

How can I be more organized in the morning and not be stressed before I even get to work?

Are those navy pants with your black jacket?

Try putting your clothes out the night before. This will avoid grabbing mix-matched clothing at the last minute before you rush out the door. I have also marked on the tags of my suits the words *Navy* or *Black* to help me distinguish between them in the dim morning light.

Be prepared

Making your lunch the night before can be a real timesaver in the morning. If you don't like sandwiches that have been in the refrigerator overnight, then get the rest of your lunch ready and make your sandwiches fresh in the morning. You can even pack the ingredients into a container and put your sandwich together when you are ready to eat it. If you like to have soup at lunchtime, bring a few cans to work and leave them there.

Have everything you need to take to work ready at the door so you can quickly grab it on your way out. This will save you time and you won't forget anything. If there is something you really need to remember and you think you will forget, put a sticky note on the door as a reminder. Also, have one spot for all your important items such as your keys and transit pass or tickets.

Zzzzzz...

Try to get to bed at a decent hour. If your favourite shows are on too late in the evening, why not *record* them. Too soon and it will be time to get up again.

Set your alarm to a reasonable time and make the decision to get out of bed. If you re-set your alarm, or snooze it, and fall back to sleep you will end up feeling groggier than if you had just gotten up on the first ring. If you give yourself enough time in the morning, it can be a relaxing time to sip your coffee and eat your toast while reading the morning paper. Reward yourself for those extra minutes. Make them something to look forward to. If you have children, take this time for yourself and get ready before waking them up.

Bus stop

Don't wait until the last minute to rush out to the bus stop or jump into your car, especially if you are going to work during rush hour. Leaving even five minutes earlier can make a big difference in traffic. If you take public transit and like to read, this can actually be an enjoyable time. Giving yourself enough time will make your commute into work less stressful. While other people are riding on the *stress mobile* you will be stress-free and enjoying your morning.

What if you have children?

It has been some time since I have had to get anyone other than myself ready in the morning, but I do remember one thing, children hate being rushed to do anything and the more you try to *make them* hurry, the harder they will resist. If you are relaxed and have things under control they are more likely to get ready rather than react to your stress.

The night before you might try helping your children pick out their clothes for the next day and laying them out in a special spot for the morning. This can help avoid the "I don't want to wear that" attitude and can become a fun family time with mom or dad.

Encourage your children to help pack their lunches the night before. Nowadays it is a little tougher to just throw a lunch together because of allergies in the schools to watch for and wanting to ensure your child's lunch is environmentally friendly and nutritious, but if you get it ready the night before when you have more time, it will be easier on everyone.

Ensure all homework, notes and books have been put in their backpacks the night before or laid out where they will be remembered.

Make sure your kids put their coats and boots or shoes in the same location all the time. This way you will know where to go to retrieve them, avoiding the *big search* when you don't have the time.

If you can remember which end to open the cereal box and are prepared, your mornings can be a productive time for everyone.

* *

TIME OUT

Suggestions anyone?

The location of your Office Suggestion Box can give you a good idea of how important it is to your organization. If it is located near the garbage can, don't expect your suggestions to be taken too seriously.

PART II – SO YOU GOT THE JOB, NOW WHAT?

Chapter 1

Becoming a Go-To Assistant

*I*t is exciting when you get the call telling you that you were selected for the job. There is a lot of work that goes into preparing for the interview and to know that you were successful is a great feeling. You will want to be the best that you can be. Here are some things you can think about as you continue in your career.

The *leave it with me* attitude

Do you want to be the kind of assistant your boss and others in the office look to when they need help because they know you will get right on it and get the job done? It is never too soon to begin or too late to start.

In the interview you were probably asked if you had initiative, but once you are in the job will you show it? Initiative can be defined as using your own judgment to make decisions and doing things without having to be told. If you have initiative, you have a plan and take the next step to accomplish the task.

Can you have too much initiative?

Be prepared to go through a learning curve. The more experience you have the sooner you will be able to take initiative, but if you are new, don't be afraid to ask questions and write the answers down. Your co-workers will usually be more than happy to pass information along so that you can become part of the team. As you begin to feel confident and gather knowledge about what is expected of you, then you will be able to make more decisions and take on tasks on your own. This is the best time to start putting together a secretarial manual.

The secretarial manual

Never underestimate the value of compiling your own secretarial manual. When you find out how to do something or who to call to get something done, write it in your manual. This will be a great resource throughout your career. You will be seen as "the person with the manual that has all the answers."

You can either start a secretarial manual in a Word document, or some people are finding that using their Contact Cards in Outlook is a great tool for storing information they need to know. If you are using your Contact Cards, a good suggestion would be to create a subfolder called Secretarial Manual to keep it separate from your other Contact Cards.

Lynn Crosbie an administrative assistant at a health research centre says, "Every time I learn something new, I write it in my manual, i.e. how to use the fax machine, information about the phone system, where the photocopier is located, who my contacts are in this position, who I can call for help, etc. If I write it down the first time, I probably won't have to ask again (which your new co-workers will appreciate)."

Become an expert

Don't always rely on the IT staff for help with software issues. Educate yourself on the software programs you use. Microsoft offers online tutorials, and there is always the Help feature. It is a great tool for finding the answers you need.

Are you comfortable using the features on your telephone? When your boss wants you to set up a conference call or forward a message, can he or she rely on you to know what to do? Take the time to read and understand the telephone user's manual and keep it handy. When your boss urgently calls you in with a question you will be able to help.

Do you use the photocopier and fax machine at a basic level or have you learned some of the advanced features? The mailroom staff are usually more than happy to help you if you want to learn more. If you do not have mailroom staff and you are the person responsible, call the company that sold the equipment to your organization and ask if they offer training.

Many of the new machines have a built in *Help* feature or show *error messages* to help you figure out where the problem is.

Sue Marsh, a team leader and busy assistant in a law firm agrees, "The bottom line is: the more you know, the better you can assist your professional and the rest of your team and it makes your work easier to do."

Delegate

Becoming a Go-To Assistant, doesn't mean you have to know everything and do it all yourself, sometimes it is just taking the task and passing it on to someone who does. One of our greatest resources can be our co-workers.

Pass it on

If you have been on the job for many years, when someone new is hired on, become a mentor. What a great way to help someone new learn the ropes. And who knows, they may teach you something as well.

As an assistant you are an important part of the team and your skills are needed to effectively complete a project or job. Become the Go-To Assistant in your office.

* * * * * * * * * * * * * * * * * * *

TIME OUT

My sister went to an eye appointment with her young daughter who had just learned her alphabet. As she was getting ready to read the eye chart, her daughter urgently whispered to her, "Mom, they mixed up the letters."

Chapter 2

Joining a Professional Association: Is it Beneficial?

I have to be honest. I joined my professional association for purely selfish reasons. I created a blog for administrative assistants and thought it would make me look more credible in my field. That was my number one reason for joining, but even that reason is a valid one. Being a member of your professional association is a smart career move.

How I found out about them?

I was doing research for some articles I was working on and stumbled across one of the admin professional association websites.[3] I was a member of this particular association at a previous employer so I did know about them and was reminded of the advantages of joining.

+ It is a great place for networking with other administrative assistants. I think it helps to have people in the same profession that you can interact with and get ideas and helpful insights from.
+ By belonging to an association you will have access to job postings in the area.
+ I found the workshops and conferences provided very useful topics and information I could use in my daily work.

---

3 IAAP's website is located at: http://www.iaap-hq.org/

+ As a writer, I enjoy reading professional magazines. I am always interested in what people are writing about in our field. Most professional associations have magazines that are a benefit of membership.

+ Professional associations encourage members to participate and advance their skills in areas like public speaking, chairing a meeting, taking minutes and serving on a board, among other things. A woman I worked with was a shy person who would never speak in public, but through the encouragement of her peers she ended up chairing a conference and doing a wonderful job. It helped to have that support system. Your professional association is a safe environment to practice skills that you may need in your workplace.

+ It definitely looks good on your resume to be a member. It will show any employer that you take your career seriously and that you consider yourself a professional.

These are only a few good reasons for joining a professional association.

Subscribing to useful e-bulletins and blogs

I find it helpful to subscribe to useful e-bulletins and blogs relating to our profession. J. Watson Associates has an e-bulletin[4] with some helpful grammar and business writing tips. It is a great tool and is quick and easy to read. Some of the other e-bulletins I have seen are busy with lots of advertising, but this one is to the point and very practical.

Lynn Gaertner-Johnston has a Business Writing blog, "Talk, tips and best picks for writers on the job"[5] that has some good information and tips in it for business writing.

These are only a few that are available. There are many others out there that are very practical and helpful. It is usually a simple matter to subscribe to these feeds and if you feel you no longer want to receive them you have the option to unsubscribe.

---

4   J. Watson Associates' website is located at: http://www.jwatsonassociates. com (accessed February 16, 2007)

5   Lynn Gaertner-Johnston's blog is located at http://www.businesswritingblog. com (accessed February 1, 2008)

Chapter 3

First Things First

*T*here are so many things we need to check when we arrive at work in the morning: voicemail, e-mail, regular mail, faxes and couriers. What should we do first?

I find it is important to check your voicemail first. E-mail can be flagged as urgent, but with voicemail you have no idea until you listen to it how important it is, so best to check that first.

Next I would suggest you check your e-mail. I usually start from the bottom up and go through the e-mails, unless something is flagged *Urgent* then I go to that right away. Be careful and watch for the same subject line because you may answer an e-mail and find another e-mail further up that says "please ignore my previous e-mail."

Faxes and couriers have to be dealt with on an *as-received* basis because people are usually sending the information that way because there is some urgency to it.

Lastly it comes down to opening and sorting the regular mail and junk mail and distributing it appropriately. Keep a recycling bin handy.

Chapter 4

Setting up "My Favourites"

I have found that it is important to set up a *My Favourites* list of useful websites to help you in your job. If you are not familiar with adding Internet favourites, here are some simple instructions:

Open the Internet and go to a site you want to add to your favourites by putting the http:// address in the search.

Once you have the website you want click on *Add to Favourites*. To put your favourites in alphabetical order, right click on your list and choose *Sort by Name*.

Here are some of *My Favourites* with their corresponding links. Some of these I use on an almost daily basis. You may find these helpful as well.

- http://www.usps.gov - United States Postal Information
- www.411.com - Telephone Number Look Up
- http://www.xe.com/ucc/ - Currency Converter
- http://dictionary.cambridge.org/ - Cambridge Online Dictionaries
- http://www.yourdictionary.com/ - Multi-Language Dictionary
- http://www.phrases.org.uk/ - The Phrase Finder
- http://www.hintsandthings.co.uk/library/meanings.htm - Words and Their Meanings
- www.AskOxford.com - Grammar/Spelling/Punctuation Help Website
- http://englishplus.com/grammar/ - The Grammar Slammer
- http://www.uottawa.ca/academic/arts/writcent/hypergrammar/grammar.html - HyperGrammar (Canadian)

- http://www.mapquest.com/directions/main.adp?bCTsettings=1 - MapQuest
- http://www.countrycallingcodes.com/ - International Phone Calling and Information
- http://www.canadapost.ca/tools/pcl/bin/advanced-e.asp - Canada Postal Code Lookup
- http://www.amanet.org/ - Educational Resource
- http://www.howstuffworks.com/ - Site That Explains How Stuff Works
- http://www.canadapost.ca/tools/pg/manual/PGaddress-e.asp#1380 608 - Abbreviations for Provinces/Territories and American States
- http://www.pch.gc.ca/progs/cpsc-ccsp/jfa-ha/index_e.cfm - Canadian Public Holidays
- http://www.opm.gov/fedhol/index.asp - American Public Holidays
- http://www.worldwidemetric.com/metcal.htm - Metric Conversion
- http://www.expedia.com - Travel: Online Travel Booking
- http://www.citysearch.com/ - City Information Around The World
- http://www.traveldocs.com/ - Obtaining Visa Requirements and International Travel Information
- http://www.hoaxbusters.com – Myths and E-Mail Hoaxes
- http://searchenginewatch.com/showPage.html?page=2156221- Major Search Engines
- http://www.google.ca/ - Google (Popular Search Engine)
- http://www.weather.com - Weather information
- http://www.timeanddate.com/date/duration.html - Calculate Duration Between Two Dates
- http://www.timeanddate.com/date/dateadd.html - Date Calculator
- http://www.worldtimezone.com/ - World Time Zone Map
- http://www.worldtimeserver.com/ - International Time Zone Information
- http://www.ups.com/tracking/tracking.html - Track UPS Shipments
- http://www.fedex.com/Tracking?cntry_code=us - Track FedEx Shipments (United States)
- http://www.fedex.ca - Track FedEx Shipments (Canada)
- http://shipnow.purolator.com/ShipOnLine/Track/Track.asp - Track Purolator Shipments

+ http://www.yellow.ca/?p_lf=R&p_lang=0&p_page=f - Yellow pages
  look up

(All links accessed January 26, 2008)

* * * * * * * * * * * * * * * * * * * *

TIME OUT

When I was a hairdresser, the last thing you wanted to hear your hairdresser say was, "Oops." Here are some things that a boss would probably
not want to hear from their assistant:

+ Uh oh!
+ Was I supposed to send that?
+ Did you mean now?
+ Sorry, I forgot.
+ I *think* that's their name?
+ Oh my goodness, I sent the e-mail to the wrong person?
+ I thought you said by regular mail...
+ Was I supposed to save that document? I threw it in the garbage.
+ I forgot to send the invitations out for the conference tomorrow.
+ I hung up by mistake.
+ Sorry, I didn't get their number?
+ I don't recall anything about that file.
+ Who?
+ My computer crashed and I lost everything.
+ Oh no, I forgot to register you.
+ Was I supposed to book a flight for today? I just phoned and there
  aren't any seats available.
+ Sorry, I remembered to do everything, but book your hotel room. Do
  you have any friends in that city?

Chapter 5

Customizing Your Toolbar

Something you might like to do when opening your new computer is to customize your Toolbar in Word. I like my Toolbar set up for my working convenience and what I am familiar with.

To customize the Toolbar in Microsoft Word do the following:

+ Select *View*
+ Select *Toolbars*
+ Select *Customize*
+ Select the *Commands Tab* and follow the drag and drop instructions in the dialogue box: To add a command to a toolbar, select a category and drag the command out of this dialog box to a toolbar.

While in *Customize*, you can remove little used icons from your toolbar as well by dragging and dropping.

A quick way to customize your Toolbar is to right click on your Toolbar area, choose *Customize* and continue as above.

You can also customize the Toolbar in Outlook, Excel and PowerPoint the same way.

To Customize the Toolbar in Microsoft 2007

+ Go to the *Customize Quick Access Toolbar* located along the top of your screen on the left hand side.
+ Click on the arrow down and choose *More Commands*.

+ Choose *Customize* and choose which commands you want to select from and select what you want to add or remove.

A quick way to customize your Toolbar in Microsoft 2007 is to right click on your Toolbar area, choose *Customize Quick Access Toolbar* and continue as above.

Tip:

Take a PrintScreen of your toolbar and print it out and keep it in a safe place. This will save you from having to re-create it from memory if for some reason you lose your settings. (See Part IV, Chapter 4 for my article "Why Doesn't the IT Person Believe Me?" for more on this).

To take a PrintScreen of your toolbar do the following:

+ While in your Word document press the *PrintScreen* key on your keyboard (usually located in the top right hand corner).*
+ Open a new document in Word and paste it in by either using Ctrl V or from your toolbar *Edit* and then choose *Paste*.**

* On the newer keyboards in order to PrintScreen you need to press the *fn* key plus the PrintScreen key (*prt sc*).

**In Word 2007 choose the *Home* tab from your toolbar, then choose *Paste*.

A good idea before pasting the PrintScreen of your toolbar into a Word document is to set your document to landscape. To set your page to landscape from the toolbar choose *File - Page Set up*. Click on the *Margin* tab. Under *Orientation* choose landscape.

To do this in Word 2007 go under the *Page Layout* tab. On *Page Setup* click the arrow down on *Orientation*, then choose *Landscape*.

* * * * * * * * * * * * * * * * * * *

TIME OUT

My sister-in-law and I used to change our children's diapers on a change mat on the floor. Our reasoning was -- "They couldn't fall off the floor."

One time when my sister-in-law was changing her son he started to pee. The stream went up onto the kitchen table and into my brother's coffee cup.

Chapter 6

The only mistakes that are bad are those you don't learn from

Fear No Typo

*I*s it just me or do you immediately cringe when your boss mentions there is a *typo* in a document?

What is a typo?

The definition of typo is a small mistake made in a document when it is typed. It is an unintentional error.

I make the most mistakes when I go back and change something and then forget to take another word out or after making a change neglect to re-read the sentence to make sure it still makes sense.

Play it again Sam

The best way to avoid these types of errors is to proofread. I wish I had a quick fix, but you can't beat proofreading, especially when you have made changes to a document. You really need to read that sentence or paragraph again. A fresh set of eyes can be helpful as well. Another assistant might be able to quickly read it over for you if you have looked at it too many times.

I have also found turning on the *Check Grammar While you Type* useful as it will highlight sentences that do not read right or have incorrect punctuation and will flag them for you.

Another useful tool is AutoCorrect. In the Options for AutoCorrect make sure you click *Replace Text as you Type* and it will automatically correct commonly misspelled words.

You also have the option to turn your *Check Grammar With Spelling* on as an added measure, but I don't find that as useful and it really slows the process down when doing a Spell Check. I do however use Spell Check on e-mails and all documents that I type.

We all make mistakes

Be as careful as you can be, but if you make a mistake, go back and make the change and go on to your next task. Don't dwell on your error.

To avoid common mistakes, I have a quick mental checklist I go through while proofing my documents.

+ Is the date correct? Especially when we change to a new year, is it the correct year?
+ Do the addressee and salutation match? It is easy when you are using an old document to have the correct addressee, but in the salutation the wrong name.
+ Do you have the correct signature line and initials? Is there a c.c. or b.c.c that you have to remember to send? If you have a blind copy, make sure b.c.c. is not typed on the original letter.
+ Check to see if it is to go by fax, courier, regular mail, registered mail or e-mail, and then make sure you send it that way.
+ Are there any enclosures? Make sure correct enclosures are included.
+ Is there a watermark on the final document and does it need to be removed before printing (i.e. Draft, Copy, etc.)?
+ In e-mail before I press Send, I check to make sure I am sending to the right person and if I say I have an attachment I make sure it is actually there and open it to verify again that it is the correct attachment.

Some mistakes are more costly than others, but when we make a mistake, and we undoubtedly will, we can learn from them and we normally won't make them again.

I think I will always cringe just a little when I hear those words "there's a typo," but proofreading and going through a mental checklist will help you make fewer mistakes.

Chapter 7

There's Nothing Wrong With Asking for Help

*W*ouldn't it be nice to have your own personal helpline when you need help and the IT person has left for the day, and you just can't figure out how to print that Excel document so it fits on one page, and of course your boss needs it urgently? Help!

I am very fortunate because I can just call my sister. She is great with software programs (self-taught) and usually knows the answer to my problems, or knows where to find it. I actually joke about it when I call her and say, "Is this the Excel Helpline?" So I asked her to write something on how she gained the skills and know-how she has in Word, PPT and Excel.

Introducing Lynn Crosbie: My Help Desk

When I first got back into the workforce, I quickly realized that a computer course was something I needed since I had never used one before. And yes, I know I am showing my age.

Initially, I could not see how the lessons they were giving me on font sizing, margins, tabs, etc. were going to help me type a letter quicker than on my trusty typewriter. I could have finished that letter in two minutes. Of course, I quickly changed my mind when I saw the many advantages of using a computer.

Even when I first starting learning, I found that I wanted to know more than they were teaching me. I investigated the various menu options and started using the *Help* command. A *Help* command is included in the Microsoft Office program menu bar. The more specific you can be with your question, the better your chances are of getting an answer. Here are a few ways you can get help.

Using the Office Assistant

On the menu bar, go to Help, Show the Office Assistant. Your Office Assistant will show up on your screen usually in the lower right-hand corner, perhaps as a paperclip, a cat or a dog. Click on your Office Assistant and you will get a pop-up that says, "Type your question here." Do as it says, i.e. type in "How do I draw a curve in Word" or "Using Shortcut Keys in Word" and then click Search. You will get several results to choose from – choose the one that is closest to what you want to do and try it out.

Using the F1 key command

Press the F1 key and type in your question. F1 works in most Microsoft programs.

Tutorials

Another way to learn more about your word processing program is to do tutorials. There are several tutorials available on the Internet. Even if you are at an advanced level, you likely don't use all of the advanced features on a daily basis and the old saying holds true, "if you don't use it, you lose it." It's up to you to keep your skills up to date. The tutorials give you a good overview of what various programs can do.

If you search on the Internet and type in the word *free tutorials* and the name of the program you want to know about, something will come up.

Go to a University website and see what they are teaching. This will give you an idea of some of the many things your program can do.

Last but not least, keeping a *network* of secretaries is the best resource. You don't have to know everything, you just need to know others that do. My network is invaluable as one of my main *Help* resources.

Chapter 8

Getting Organized and Staying that Way

*N*obody likes a desk that is cluttered and disorganized with sticky notes all over the place, files here and there and papers, papers, papers. In order to function efficiently as an administrative assistant you must be organized. When my desk is not organized I begin to feel buried and out of control.

To keep myself organized I have a place on my desk for everything. If it has to do with accounting, I have a bin for that. If it has to do with scheduling meetings, I have another bin for that. And if it has to do with waiting, waiting on an answer, waiting for a return phone call, whatever I may be waiting on, I have a *Wait Bin* for that.

Having a place for everything and routinely using it will keep you organized and when you get a phone call about a meeting or your boss has an urgent request, if you get into the routine of using these special bins you will know to go right to your *Scheduling Bin* or your *Wait Bin*. It will make your work life much easier.

When your boss sees you in control, then he or she can relax and know that you will be able to look after the matter.

Trying to remember

We can't remember everything and therefore it is essential to have reminder systems to keep on top of things.

Using the bring-forward system

The Bring-Forward System (or sometimes referred to as a BF system) might be an old term for the younger assistant, but the principle is similar to using your Tasks in Outlook. You need to have some sort of system to bring forward items that need to be handled at a future date. Putting a reminder in your Outlook Tasks and then putting the document you need to bring forward in your Wait Bin is a good way to bring forward items.

Some assistants still use the old-fashioned method of writing on index cards in a card box with monthly and daily dividers and they check it each day for items or files that need to be brought forward for attention. The advantage I find to this system is you actually have a hard copy to look at and if your system goes down you are still able to function effectively.

Whatever system you use, having a good bring-forward system is important so you do not miss important dates or timelines.

Using your Tasks in Outlook

In a busy office sometimes your automatic task reminders are the only way you can remember all the things you need to do.

To set a task reminder in Outlook:

- File - New - Task (or Ctrl - Shift - K).
- Type in the Subject or Task.
- Set the Task date and Reminder date. It is important to click on the Reminder check-box and set when you want to be reminded so that you actually get sent the task reminder.
- Use the space provided to make any notes, i.e. where files are located, e-mails, etc. to complete the task.

When you set the start date, it automatically sets the due date as the same date, which is probably what you want.

The importance of the to-do list

Whether you are organizing a large conference or managing your daily tasks, a to-do list is essential.

Keeping a handy notepad by your phone and writing things down throughout the day is just smart. When you have completed an item, strike it off the list. A good idea would also be to bring a notepad and a pen with you when you are called into your boss's office to take any notes or instructions down. Yellow sticky notes are also an option. You can write instructions on them and put it on the file or correspondence as a reminder of what you need to do. Some assistants also carry small notepads and pens with them when they are away from their desk.

When organizing a conference you will need a more extensive to-do list. Write down everything you will need to do to arrange the conference, from booking the venue, to ordering supplies, sending out invitations, or whatever you need to do and list them in order with a checklist so you can keep track of when an item is completed or needs to be done. Check your to-do list daily to make sure you are on top of things and nothing has been forgotten. Putting your to-do list in a table format is probably the easiest way to set it up and putting corresponding Tasks in Outlook is a good follow up system to your to-do list.

See Part V, Chapter 2 for information on *Organizing a Conference* and using a to-do list. At the end of that chapter there is a sample to-do list.

I hate filing

Keeping up with your filing is one of the most important things you can do to keep yourself organized. There is nothing worse than madly looking on your desk and wracking your brain wondering where that piece of paperwork is – especially when your boss needs it urgently. Having a good workable filing system and an organized and uncluttered desk is critical to staying organized.

Filing on a daily basis is the best way to keep on top of your filing, but sometimes your busy workday does not permit that ideal goal. A good suggestion to clear your desk of filing in the short term is to take a legal-sized accordion bellows and insert tabs from A to Z. You can put individual filing in alphabetical order by client name or topic in the appropriate tab. This will get the filing off your desk and put in a place where it can be easily managed. When you have some down time you can do your filing from the bellows.

The advantage to this system is if your boss needs something quickly, you can go to the bellows and easily retrieve it from the appropriate tab as opposed to going through the pile of filing on your desk and hoping you find it quickly.

Maintaining an up-to-date file list is also a necessary tool to keep everything in order. It shouldn't be too complicated and should be something that others could look at and use. Sometimes things happen and someone has to fill in for you, so you want something easy to follow. A Word document with an alphabetical listing of all your files is probably the easiest way to do it.

You also need to keep your electronic filing systems organized. Especially as we look to a paperless society we need to keep our folders and subfolders organized in our document management system and in Outlook. But all is not lost if we can't remember where it is filed, because in Outlook and in most document management systems we can search all folders and still come up with our document. So in that sense, filing electronically has its advantages.

When filing electronically, the name of the document and key words become important to finding documents and if you can save by file number that narrows the search down even further.

The miscellaneous file

There are some things in your physical files as well as your electronic files that just don't seem to have a home. They tend to get put in the Miscellaneous file and that is OK as long as you are consistent and always put that type of thing in there. Sometimes on my file list under Miscellaneous I will put in brackets a word that will help me in my search if I need to find it later.

What works for me, may not work for you, but the important thing is to have some kind of system in place that will enable you to find things, and help you keep track of dates and important tasks.

Outlook tip when searching for e-mails

In Outlook (2007) in the Search field there is a drop-down menu. Choose *Search All Mail Items*. Type what you are looking for and Outlook will search in all your folders.

What a great tool when you can't remember where you filed an e-mail.

Chapter 9

What is Metadata and Why is it Important for the Assistant to Know About it?

I overheard some assistants talking in the locker room at the gym. They were saying their IT person was bugging them about metadata. They concluded they were not going to worry about it and would press the Delete button on the IT person's e-mail warning. They reasoned if they didn't understand it, there was nothing they had to do.

Should we be concerned?

Metadata is defined as *data about data.* It is basically information embedded in a document that can tell a user information about how the document was created, including information your company may not want someone else to see.

The Government of Canada, Office of the Privacy Commissioner, has developed a fact sheet on metadata and the risks and how to minimize those that I would recommend every assistant read.[6] I think it would be a good site to visit for information, no matter what country you are from. We all have metadata to deal with.

---

6 Government of Canada, Office of the Privacy Commissioner, *The Risks of Metadata,* http://www.privcom.gc.ca/fs-fi/02_05_d_30_e.asp (accessed January 26, 2008)

What are some of the risks?

Hidden text that is not visible to you is actually visible in metadata. What you thought you were writing in private *for your eyes only* is visible to anyone who checks the metadata. Someone who checks the metadata will also know all the revisions made and deleted. This could be potentially embarrassing, or worse, to your company.

Any comments that were put on a document, even though you deleted them, are still embedded in the metadata. For instance your boss could have put a comment, "Find out how this is done?" as a note to himself to do some research on a subject. This could be embarrassing to your organization if not seen in the proper context, especially if it is written in a document being sent to a potential client.

If you use a previously saved document as a template for a new document, all the old information is still embedded in the metadata, including company name, personal information, medical information, financial details and customer, client or patient names.

There could be financial risks to your organization by overlooking metadata. Fines and financial penalties could be levied and your company could lose a potential client. I read an interesting article called "Hit send... and regret it" and got a better idea how serious this could be to you and your organization.[7]

When your IT Department sends an e-mail alerting you to the dangers of metadata and what you need to do as an assistant to minimize the risk to your organization -- do not press Delete. Read it and act on it. Ask your IT Department what they want you to do to protect your organization against this risk.

---

7   Ferguson, Iain, ZDNet Australia, Hit *send...and regret it*, at http://www. zdnet.com.au/news/communications/soa/Hit_send_and_regret_it/0,200006179 1,39220866,00.htm (accessed January 26, 2008)

Chapter 10

To Shred or Not to Shred: Disposing of Confidential Documents

I attended an IAAP dinner meeting where we had a lawyer speak to us about the proper disposal of confidential documents. As assistants we often work with information that is confidential and we need to use good practices when disposing of these documents.

In Canada document disposal came to the attention of Ontario's Privacy Commissioner in the filming of a mini-series in Toronto. The Toronto Star reported that as filmmakers were re-enacting events about the 9/11 terrorist attacks, documents were strewn on downtown streets as *fake garbage*. It was discovered that some of these were confidential medical records.[8]

Garbage that was earmarked for shredding at a clinic instead went to a recycling company where it was sold to the film company. As the papers were blowing in the wind a reporter grabbed one of these documents, which happened to be a confidential medical record and the ball started to roll from there.

Privacy is serious business in Canada and the companies involved were held accountable. Imagine being the employees involved in this situation? Our actions can have consequences, including where we put our garbage.

---

8 Toronto Star, *Film shoot uses real medical records*, October 2, 2005 (used with permission)

Here are some guidelines that assistants can keep in mind when disposing of documents:

+ If you have any doubt whatsoever shred it or put it in locked shredding bins.
+ Recycling is NOT a secure disposal mechanism. Any document sent to be recycled could be publicly sold and used, as happened in the case noted above.
+ Placing a document in a garbage bin is NOT a secure disposal mechanism.
+ Cleaning staff do not distinguish between documents for recycling and those to be sent for shredding. Don't think that because you have For Shredding Only written on the box that this will solve the problem. Some cleaning staff may not be able to read and understand English. They just see a box of paper garbage. Don't assume your instructions will be followed.
+ Beware putting a recycling bin at a common printer as sensitive documents could easily be put in there by mistake.
+ Never leave any sensitive documents in a car or trunk, even if the vehicle is locked. This also includes while running into the store for a few minutes to pick up an item. It only takes a minute for someone to break into your vehicle and steal a laptop or other confidential work information.
+ Never recycle sensitive documents at home.

With the new privacy laws in Canada, and privacy consciousness everywhere, it is even more important to follow good disposal practices for confidential and sensitive documents.

The lawyer who spoke to us also brought up privacy issues when we talk about confidential work issues with our spouse or when we bring work home and leave it around the house for anyone to see. Do we consider that our children may unwittingly share confidential work information that they might see or hear us talking about on a social networking site such as Facebook? When we sign our employment confidentiality agreement it obviously doesn't stop when we leave the building.

Gone are the days when privacy simply meant closing our doors and drawing the shades. We need to read our work privacy policies and make sure we are following them.

Chapter 11

Colour Blindness:
Does it Matter to the Assistant?

A friend of mine who works for a research hospital was preparing a PPT presentation for a doctor and used red to highlight a point. The doctor told her that she should never use red because there are a significant number of men who have trouble seeing red. I had never heard of that before so I decided to do some research on it and indeed that is the case.

The Howard Hughes Medical Institute (HHMI) report that, "some 10 million American men – fully 7 percent of the male population – either cannot distinguish red from green, or see red and green differently from most people. This is the commonest form of color blindness, but it affects only .4 percent of women."[9] The statistics are comparable in other countries of the world.

How does this relate to us as assistants?

I would not recommend using red font for a PPT presentation. I would also suggest that using red to emphasize words in an e-mail would not be appropriate. The HHMI report goes on to state that it is very rare for anyone to be blind to the blue end of the colour spectrum. I would, however, suggest that the best choice is black on a white background.

---

9   Howard Hughes Medical Institute, *Color Blindness: More Prevalent Among Males*, (1995 report) (Accessed February 2, 2008) (Used with permission)

If you want something to stand out, rather than using a colour you can always use **bold** or *italics* for emphasis. I would not use underlining for emphasis in an electronic document as underlining a word usually means it is a link to something else. Since underlining has taken on this new meaning you may have some confused readers trying to link to another site.[10]

In the background

I did a search on the Internet and came up with many sites that discuss the problems web designers have when designing sites that will be reader friendly for all users. This includes fonts, but also the choice of background colour. Many designers take colour blindness into consideration when designing WebPages, but we should also keep it in mind when choosing colours for PPT presentations, e-mail font choices and background wallpaper colours.[11]

---

10 Gaertner-Johnston, Lynn, Business Writing "Talk, tips, and best picks for writers on the Job," *Underlining: A Bad Choice Online*, http://www.businesswriting-blog.com/business_writing/2008/02/underlining-a-b.html (accessed February 16, 2008)

11 About.com, *Are Your Web Pages Color Sensitive? Color Blindness Can Make Your Web Pages Unusable*, http://webdesign.about.com/od/accessibility/a/aa062804.htm, (accessed February 2, 2008)

Chapter 12

Thinking Outside the Job Description Box

Today's assistants are computer savvy, smart and up-and-coming, and consider themselves professionals in the workplace. They are no longer stuck within the job description box, but have the freedom to break out of the mould and redefine their roles and sometimes even change their careers.

Employers have begun to recognize our changing roles in the workplace and some have reflected that by changing our title from *secretary* to titles that more accurately describe the positions we are performing in our organizations such as:

- Legal Assistant
- Personal Assistant or Personal Aide
- Medical Assistant
- Executive Assistant
- Office Coordinator or Office Manager

Administrative assistants are highly skilled in many areas and sometimes we take it for granted, not recognizing where we could go with our skills. Here are some ideas to get you thinking in that direction.

Event planning

Event planning is a big industry that looks for people who are skilled in planning big events without a hitch. What better candidate to take on that role as a career than the assistant who regularly plans events from small meetings to large conferences.

Marketing

An assistant who has a marketing flare with a creative mind can branch out into editing or writing. Those who are skilled at regularly thinking on their feet as they come up with solutions and ideas both on the computer and on the job might be able to step into this role.

Some examples would be managing a company website, creating, editing and writing a company newsletter or creating promotional materials, invitations and brochures for marketing events. This can be a rewarding career change for those suited to this type of work.

Finance

An assistant with a head for numbers may be able to move into finance in an accounting or tax firm. Some assistants regularly manage small budgets when planning functions or have bookkeeping responsibilities and work regularly on spreadsheets. Those with experience in this area might enjoy this type of career move.

Professional organizer

Organization is a must if you are an assistant. One of our main duties is to keep our bosses organized. While being organized seems natural to us because of the nature of our jobs, some people are not and need help and are looking for skilled and organized people to do the job for them.

Working within your current job

Someone who wants to remain in their administrative assistant position but spread their wings, can work with their supervisor and HR Manager to develop and change their role by specializing in certain areas and do more of the things they enjoy and are good at.

Administrative assistants have a list of things they specialize in including business writing, proofreading, minute taking, meeting planning, travel agent, desktop publishing, editing, public relations and client liaison to name a few.

Some assistants have expanded their role to that of an executive assistant which sometimes means performing the role of an office manager.

Working our way out of a job

Kim began as an administrative assistant and has now become the HR Director of a major law firm.

Sue is an IT specialist who started out as an administrative assistant with a knack for computers and made it work for her as a career.

Elizabeth began as an administrative assistant in an accounting firm and has become a junior chartered accountant.

What do these three women have in common?

- They each had a desire to pursue a different area of interest and they changed their direction and worked themselves into a new career.
- They each had forward-thinking employers who allowed them to have vision and encouraged them to work towards their goal and made room for that new role within their organization.
- They each took the initiative to get appropriate training and education to better equip them in the areas they were interested in.

Our jobs are not limited to just being a *secretary*. We may need to look at courses that will help us reach our goals, but the possibilities can be endless when we think outside the box.

* * * * * * * * * * * * * * * * * * *

TIME OUT

You said what?

Spell Check never replaces proofreading a document. I have proofed documents in which the person has relied only on Spell Check and the outcome has been comical. A few examples of this are: A lawyer writing to a potential client writes that he has *expensive* experience, instead of *extensive* experience. I remember reading a document and instead of *its* they had written *tits*.

Bloopers to be sure, funny yes, but professional – NO! Be sure you always proofread your document and then Spell Check it as an extra step to your proofreading.

PART III – OFFICE MANNERS

Chapter 1

What to do About Unwelcome E-mails?

I t is always difficult to know what to do when a friend or co-worker sends you lengthy joke e-mails or funny pictures and chain e-mails at work. You don't want to hurt their feelings, but if you are like me you just don't have time for them at the office. I personally don't even like receiving most of them at home, unless they are sent personally to me by a friend and it is something they know I will get a chuckle out of or that I am interested in. Sometimes when I get these e-mails I feel it was just a *forward to all my address book* type of mailing and the person didn't personally have me in mind when they were sending it.

Here are some rules I go by:

1. Never send joke e-mails, chain e-mails or joke photos to anyone's work e-mail account. If you feel the need to send them, send them to a home e-mail account instead (I can't stress this enough).

2. When you pass something on for the first time, why don't you ask your friend if they mind you sending it to them and to feel free to let you know if they would prefer not receiving these types of e-mails. Don't feel offended if they answer you in the negative though. After all, you did ask.

3. If I am passing on an e-mail, I do not send it to my whole address book, but only a select few who might appreciate it, others may not. When I forward an e-mail, I send a personal message letting them

know why I thought they might get a kick out of the message or photo I am passing on to them.

4. I clean up the e-mail I am forwarding and take out the string of e-mail addresses. We don't need to read who forwarded it to whom and have to scroll down before we see why it was sent to us.

5. I also delete the last paragraph that says *unless I forward this to all my friends something bad will happen* as I don't want my friends to feel they have to do that or for them to think that is why I am forwarding it to them.

6. If I receive e-mails from friends with *dire warnings*, when I reply to them I usually look up their particular warning to show them it is a hoax[12] and that usually encourages them to do the same before forwarding these types of things on again.

Pardon the interruption

I received an e-mail recently with the introduction *Pardon the interruption* and thought that was a good opening for an e-mail that may or may not apply to everyone in your organization, but must be sent to all for convenience sake and expediency. It made me feel the person was concerned about interrupting me and it made the e-mail seem less intrusive.

----

12 www.hoaxbusters.com

Chapter 2

When Using Your Cell Phone Can Be Bad Manners

Our technology is moving ahead full speed, but it seems our etiquette is lagging behind. Every time we turn around there's another article on etiquette. Why does all our good etiquette sense go out the window just because we are on a cell phone?

Some employers are even considering banning cell phone use at work because of our poor manners.

What is it about the cell phone that we just *have* to run for it when it rings? Why does it seem so urgent when we get a call on our cells that we interrupt our conversations to answer it? Is our technology moving ahead of our good manners?

Soap opera transit

A phone rings on the bus and everyone looks down and reaches for their cell. There are a lot of conversations going on, but no one is talking to each other, we are all on our cells.

Think about what you are saying on your cell and what people are hearing. Does everyone really need to hear about all your troubles with your boyfriend or girlfriend and more importantly, do you really want everyone to know all your private business?

Remember everyone can hear your phone conversations when you are on a cell. Consider this, are you unknowingly leaking confidential work information, not realizing you have a busload of people listening in on your conversation? This may be a breach of your confidentiality agreement with your employer. Be careful.

Smile you're on Candid Camera.

Camera phones are banned in locker rooms and change rooms in gyms for obvious reasons. It is an invasion of our privacy. What about in the workplace or on public transit? Never take someone's picture without their knowledge or consent. In the workplace it is a definite no-no.

Is that your phone ringing?

Some people have set their phone rings to some pretty strange ring tones: A baby crying, someone screaming, the whole chorus of Dancing Queen and others. When their cell phone rings they wait for the whole ring to be completed. Why do we have to hear your whole cell phone ring? Please just answer the phone!

Practice good manners

Use good manners when using your cell phone. You would not think it good manners if someone butted into your conversation with your co-worker, so treat your cell phone the same way. It can wait. Or if you are waiting for an urgent call, excuse yourself and say this is an urgent call that you've been waiting for and you must take it.

Text messaging

Text messaging when you are having a conversation with someone is like *talking behind their back*. How would you feel if while in a conversation with someone the person you are with was texting a message to someone else - perhaps even about you.

Can't you see I'm on the phone?

Actually No! With the increasing use of hands-free cell phones in the office and on the street it is often impossible to tell if someone is on the phone.

We have all seen it. Someone is walking down the street involved in an animated conversation seemingly with themselves and then you notice they are talking on a hands-free cell phone. Or your boss is in their office on a hands-free cell and you start to speak to him or her and they wonder why you are interrupting their telephone call.

Hands-free cell phones are convenient. They have ergonomic advantages, but people who use them tend to forget that the rest of us can't always tell when they are on the phone.

We need to be patient with each other as we learn to adapt to new technologies and be aware of the challenges they pose.

Cell phone technology is great. The conveniences are endless and being able to conduct business on a cell phone when you can't be at the office is good for business. But let's not forget our manners. Good cell phone etiquette is just using your common sense and good manners on the way to work, at work and at home.

Chapter 3

The E-tiquette of E-mail

E -mail is no longer just for personal use, with all our accepted short forms: LOL, U, GB and a co-worker's favourite, OMG! With the increasing use of e-mail as the first choice for business correspondence it opens a whole new world of do's and don'ts for the assistant.

Here are some good-sense e-mail etiquette tips

E-mail salutations

Although e-mail is less formal than writing a letter it is still polite to open with a greeting. For external business e-mails I would suggest Hello or Hi. Dear is too formal in North America, but in European and Asian countries it is appropriate and proper.

Be courteous with e-mail!

Are you there?

Who hasn't been annoyed when you e-mail someone and are waiting for an answer, only to find out the person is on vacation, but didn't put their Out-of-Office Assistant on. It is important to let people know when you will not be in the office.

For those who are unfamiliar with the Out-of-Office Assistant, go under *Tools, Out-of-Office Assistant.*

The following information should be included in your message:

1) The start and end dates of your absence.
2) A message to let your contacts know you will answer messages when you return.
3) The name, contact information, and office hours of someone to contact if they require immediate assistance. *Of course, be sure to check with your co-worker first before providing his or her information.*

Who are you?

Be sure to add your signature to your business e-mail with your coordinates. Your company may have a policy on what they want you to include in the signature line and what it should look like, but generally you would include your name, title, company name and address, telephone, fax number and e-mail address.

To set an e-mail signature file:

1) From the *Tools* menu, choose *Options*.
2) Select *Mail Format*.
3) Select *Signatures*.
4) Select *New* and follow the instructions to add your e-mail signature. You can make more than one signature to use for different e-mails.
5) If you want your signature to be applied automatically to new messages and for replies and forwards. Go back to *Mail Format* and you will see a drop-down menu for *Signature for new message* and *Signature for replies and forwards*. You need to select the signature you want applied to these functions or leave at *None* if you do not want this set.

Saying thank you

It can be irritating to get an e-mail only to open it and all it says is *Thank you*, but it is also good manners to reply to an e-mail to say thank you and to acknowledge receipt and end the conversation. A good suggestion by Jane Watson[13] is to reply to the e-mail and put *Thank you* in the subject line and write *(End)* after it. This way they will know they do not need to open the message. An example would be: Thank you (End) Re: Letter to J. Richards.

---

13   J. Watson Associates' website is located at: http://www.jwatsonassociates.com (accessed February 16, 2007)

DON'T SHOUT!

Writing all in caps is a form of e-mail shouting. Is that the message you want to send to your recipient?

If you are visually impaired and need to use all caps and large font and don't want to offend the reader, state that in your opening sentence. That way the reader can relax and continue to read the e-mail knowing you are not shouting at them.

Seeing red

Does it matter what colour of font you use in your e-mail? Colour blindness affects a significant number of people, especially men, when it comes to distinguishing the colour red and green. (See Part II – Chapter 11, *Colour Blindness: Does it Matter to the Assistant?*)

If you want something to stand out, rather than using a colour try using **bold** or *italics* for emphasis.

What about all that pretty wallpaper that is available for your background? Be sure to check your company e-mail policy: Having butterflies flutter across the screen on the opening of the business e-mail may not be the image your company is looking for.

Reply to all

If you are copied on an e-mail and want to respond to the sender, is it really necessary to *Reply to all* and have all of the recipients receive your e-mail? If your message is an answer to the sender then just pressing *Reply* is appropriate or if you are only copied on the e-mail, do you need to reply at all?

Be angry but send not!

It is too easy to press *Send* and then regret what you have written or find yourself in some legal trouble.

If you need to vent try sending *yourself* the e-mail you wanted to send. Take a few moments to calm down and then go to your Inbox and open your message. You will get a greater sense of what impact that e-mail will have on the recipient. But it is never a good idea to send an angry e-mail in business correspondence.

Good grammar, spelling and punctuation

The rules still apply for using good grammar and punctuation in e-mail. Are you starting that new sentence using a capital letter? Are you asking a question or stating a fact? Is this a new paragraph? Your e-mail will be easier to read if you follow some basic business writing rules.

Read the e-mail over for completeness and accuracy. Spell Check never replaces proofreading your e-mail.

If you say in your e-mail that you have an attachment, is the attachment actually there? And please verify to make sure the attachment is the correct attachment, it is easy to drag and drop the wrong one.

Check the name of the recipient. Make sure they are the actual person (people) you want to send to. Some names are similar in your contact list and it is easy to choose the wrong person, which, depending on the sensitivity of the e-mail, could be embarrassing or worse.

Mixed messages

If you are changing the subject, please do not reply to the old e-mail with the same subject line. This can get confusing for the recipient. A good rule of thumb is if you change the subject, start a new e-mail message.

In our fast-paced society, e-mail is a quick way of communicating and used properly, can be an effective business tool, but e-mail can also be impersonal and is not always the best form of communication. Sometimes a better way to communicate would be picking up the phone or meeting someone face to face.

Think twice before pressing *Send*. Is e-mail the best way to communicate your message?

Tip for filing e-mails

If it is necessary to file a hard copy of the e-mail, file it chronologically by date and time. This will make it easier for the reader to follow the chain of e-mails.

Chapter 4

Voicemail is a Two-Way Street

I called someone on their business phone and their voicemail greeting said, "Leave a message and I'll get right back to you," but they didn't identify who they were. I had never met the person so had no idea by that message if I had the correct number. As a joke a co-worker suggested leaving the message, "Hi, call me back."

Recording your message

A good tip I was given by a co-worker, as she heard me fumbling my way trying to record my voicemail greeting, was to write it out beforehand and then read it when recording it. The following should be included in your greeting:

- Your name, title and who you work for, but you could also include your company name.
- You should let people know if you are in that day and, if so, that you will return the call when you return to your desk.
- If you are on a planned time off you should give the dates you will be away and leave the name of someone to contact in your absence. Please don't dead-end your voicemail! Just because you are on vacation doesn't mean your company is. Sometimes your phone number or e-mail address is the only contact a person has to your organization. Please refer them to someone else in your absence.

+ If you are on an unplanned day off you have the option of changing your own voicemail message from home, or you can have a co-worker do it on your behalf.
+ Consider using the temporary out of office voicemail greeting. This way you don't have to change your original message each time and it automatically comes off on the date and time you want.
+ A suggested voicemail greeting would be: "Hello. You have reached the voicemail of [name, title]. I am either on the phone or away from my desk. Please leave a message and I will return your call as soon as possible."

Leaving a message

One day, my sister picked up her voicemail messages to learn that she had five messages. She got her pen and paper ready only to find out that each message was a *hang-up*. She wondered who was trying to get in touch with her, but couldn't do much about it since a message wasn't left. She got home that night to her husband telling her that he had been trying to reach her and he wondered where she had been all day.

+ Please don't hang up, or if you prefer not to leave a message, hang up before the beep so the person doesn't have to go to the trouble of retrieving the message only to get a hang up.
+ State your name, number and the purpose for your call. If you leave the purpose for your call, many times when they return the call, they can leave the information you need on your voicemail. This avoids telephone tag.
+ I personally like it when people leave the date and time of their call, however, there is always the option of turning on the date and time stamp on your voicemail.
+ Repeat your phone number at the end of your voicemail, especially if you are calling from a cell phone. Cell phones are not as clear as land lines and it is sometimes hard to make out what the person is saying.

Chapter 5

Swearing in the Workplace

I have read articles that swearing in the workplace is good for you and helps to relieve stress[14] and have read other articles that swearing in the workplace can be cause for disciplinary action or possibly even get you fired.[15]

I have worked in offices where there was zero tolerance for swearing and I have worked in other offices where swearing was common and acceptable. There seems to be some controversy on this issue, but I personally think swearing is inappropriate for the office and comes across as unprofessional and would not recommend it.

No matter what your position is on this issue I would suggest you check your office policy to make sure you are in compliance. If your office policy states there is zero tolerance for swearing you need to check your language at the door and be aware of what you are saying as it could affect your career.

---

14 NetWorkWorld, *Never mind the b******t, swearing at work is a good thing,* http://www.networkworld.com/community/node/20718 (accessed January 28, 2008)

15 New York Times, *The 4-Letter-Word Patrol is in Pursuit,* http://query.nytimes.com/gst/fullpage.html?res=950CE0D81130F934A15755C0A9679C8B 63&sec=&spon=&pagewanted=all (accessed January 28, 2008)

Chapter 6
Chatty People: Getting Back to Business

You are trying to get an important project completed and a co-worker comes along wanting to chat. I am sure we have all experienced this at one time or another. How can you handle it and continue to have good working relationships with your co-workers?

There is always going to be some social interaction and joking in the office. It can help to relieve some of the stress of a busy office. After all, we spend most of our time with the people at work and we want to develop good working relationships with each other in order to work more effectively together, but sometimes we urgently need to get back to work.

A good suggestion if someone is settling in for a long chat would be to try some body language and stand up. Standing up shows you need to go somewhere. That body language may be enough to get the message across.

You can try continuing to work as they are chatting and they should get the hint. If all else fails you may just need to tell them you are busy and really have to get back to the task at hand, but you would be happy to talk to them at lunch or a break.

What if you are the chatterer? Try to recognize the signs that your co-worker does not have time to chat right now. Don't take it personally if they need to continue working and can't talk. We are at work to do a job and that is our first priority. Socializing can come at lunch time, breaks or work-related social get-togethers.

Chapter 7

Difficult Working Relationships

I have often joked with my co-workers that this world would be an easier place to live in if it weren't for the people. People can be difficult at times. I can be difficult at times.

I heard a speaker say that the way you handle conflict depends on your experiences and I believe that is true. Managing conflict with limited knowledge and skill in that area will most likely not result in success. I am the type of person who believes in the *do unto others as you would have them do unto you* rule, so when someone breaks that and does something that I wouldn't even think of doing I find it hard to know how to deal with it.

When I hear someone speak or I read a book and the author is skilled in the area of conflict management, I get good ideas and tools for dealing with conflicts and it is very helpful. I think we need to be equipped to handle situations that come up at work and at home.

I heard someone speak recently on managing conflict and it prompted some good discussions and insight into this topic by the participants.

We were given the five types of conflict style and asked to determine which type we were.

- The avoider does not want to have confrontation and will do anything they can to avoid it.
- The competitor wants to win. It is a competition with them and sometimes they will try to win at all costs. The relationship is not as important as the goal.

- The accommodator plays the role of the mediator. They try to smooth any ruffled feathers. The relationship is very important to them.
- The compromiser wants negotiation and compromise. They want things to be resolved such that everyone wins.
- The collaborator seeks a solution that is good for everyone. They look at the issues, not the personalities involved in the conflict.

It was an interesting workshop as we went through different scenarios and tried to determine which type of conflict style would be best in that particular situation. We also had to give our reasons why we would choose that particular style. We could see that in different situations, different styles needed to be used.

People who are skilled in conflict management can break it down for us and then we can see clearer what needs to be done. Bob Wall has written an excellent book on the subject.[16] It is very interesting and details conflicts and how they can be resolved. Of course it makes perfect sense when it happens to someone else, but it is more difficult when it is a situation you are dealing with at your own work or home.

We will all have difficult situations to deal with at one time or another and having knowledge and know-how to approach them is a good first step.

* * * * * * * * * * * * * * * * * * *

TIME OUT

The boss that hovers

Don't you just hate it when your boss stands behind you as you are trying to get something urgently done? I make all sorts of mistakes as I try to type with someone looking on. I can almost hear them anxiously pacing in their minds, "Hurry up, hurry up!"

---

16 Wall, Bob, *Working Relationships: The Simple Truth About Getting Along with Friends and Foes at Work*

Chapter 8

Leaving Your Job

*I*f you have to leave a job no matter the reason, make sure you do it with professionalism. It is never a good idea to burn bridges.

I give two weeks' notice and make myself available to help in the transition period as much as I can. If there is an overlap I offer to train the new person.

I was once laid off as a result of government downsizing, but that is still no excuse for being unprofessional. I wanted to leave on good terms and to be able to use the time I was in the position as a positive experience and a positive reference. When you leave a position it is a good time to ask for a reference letter for your records.

What if you are fired?

Some good advice from Richard Moran, author of *Nuts, Bolts & Jolts* is, "If you get fired, give yourself two days at most to feel sorry for yourself. Focus on your next job, not your last one."[17]

We can spend too much time trying to figure out what happened. If there are things you need to work on, try focussing on that and on improving your performance. Sometimes it is just personality types that don't work and it has nothing to do with your performance, or maybe the job was not the right fit for you. Whatever the reason, Mr. Moran's advice is the best I've seen. Look forward to your next job, not back on your old one.

---

17 Moran, Richard A., Author, *Nuts, Bolts & Jolts* (used with permission)

Chapter 9
Cross-Border Spelling

I use Canadian English and quite frankly I did not even think about it until I started exchanging e-mails with someone in the States and they remarked on my spelling of certain words. I write *My Favourites* whereas in the States they would write *My Favorites*. However the Internet is without borders and because of that we are doing business back and forth between countries more frequently and with greater ease.

Does it matter?

As a Canadian, when I receive correspondence from the States and I notice their way of spelling a word it is not a big deal, as phonetically it is still the same word. I think, however, as a common courtesy if you are writing to someone in English outside of your country it would be correct to spell in their *language*. In particular, if a Canadian company is corresponding with an American company I would take the extra step of writing in American English and vice versa.

Watch your Language – Settings

The default language setting in Microsoft Word is English (United States). I would suggest that Canadians set the default to Canadian English. If you are creating a document that needs to be sent to the States you could set the language to English (United States) and do a Spell Check and it would automatically pick up all the Canadian words as errors so you could easily change it to the American spelling.

To set your language in Microsoft Word 2007, go under the *Review* tab, under *Proofing*, and choose *Set Language*. Click on the language you want to use and at the bottom you have the option of setting this language as your default. If *Set Language* is not in your current proofing options you will have to add it by right clicking and choose *Customize Quick Access Toolbar* and add *Set Language*. The *Customize Quick Access Toolbar* is located along the top of your screen and you will see an icon for *Set Language*.

If you are using an older version of Microsoft Word, from the Toolbar under *Tools*, choose *Language - Set Language*. Click on the language you want to use and at the bottom you have the option of setting this language as your default.

I would do the same when sending documents to other English-speaking countries. It is an easy process to change the language and if you look in your *Set Language* under English you will notice quite a large selection of English dictionaries: United States, Belize, South African and United Kingdom to name a few.

* * * * * * * * * * * * * * * *

TIME OUT

Keeping Mr. and Mrs. Smith together

A quick way to keep words together in a Word document is to use the Shortcut Keys.

I never like to split a name up in a letter, i.e. Mr. and Mrs. Smith.

Instead of pressing the Spacebar after *Mrs.* press Shift Ctrl Spacebar and then type Smith.

Mr. and Mrs. Smith will now stay together.

PART IV – TEAMBUILDING

Chapter 1

The Secretarial Network: Working Together

I n all my years as a secretary I have found that having a network of assistants has been a tremendous help when I just can't figure out how to word that sentence in the letter my boss has asked me to send or I am wondering where to find the information I urgently need, or even, "Do you know of any openings? I have to get out of this job." What a help it is knowing I have these people I can e-mail or phone to get an answer to my dilemma in minutes. Of course when you are dealing with other assistants outside of your office keep in mind your employer's business is confidential and when you are asking questions you should keep things very general and not give specific details about a matter.

The other secretaries you work with in your own organization can be your greatest resource. Treat them with respect and you will find a wealth of information and help.

Sometimes it seems my boss thinks *I know all things*, but he doesn't know my secret...and that is my secretarial network.

Chapter 2

Will You Be My Buddy?
The Importance of Teamwork

*W*e have all seen it in job postings, "Must be able to work well in a team environment." How important is it that we are team players in the workplace?

In sports it is easy to see that working as a team is the way to win the game. How many of us as we are anxiously watching a sporting event are yelling at the television set, "Get your act together guys, you are all over the place. You will never win the game that way." Or at least that's what I'm yelling at my television set.

It is the same principle in the office. I believe that working as a team will not only increase productivity, but will give each of the team members a feeling of accomplishment while working towards a common goal, but if you are "all over the place" then nobody wins.

Meeting together as a team

In any company large or small it is important for staff to meet together. If you work for a large organization it can be even more important as size alone can make communication difficult. The different areas of your organization are all playing a part in getting a job done and in order for that to work smoothly you need to communicate with each other so each of the team members are aware of what will be required of them.

The team model from one office I worked in was the best I have seen, especially when it came to the assistant. They recognized the importance of the assistant in accomplishing their goals. We had regular team meetings and in each Department one assistant was assigned the Team Leader role to represent the assistants in their group. The meetings included administrative assistants, the Office Manager, team leaders from the service areas like the Mailroom, IT Department, Finance, Reception, etc.

Each team leader was responsible for speaking to their team members before the meeting to find out what items they wanted brought up, what jobs were coming up and what assistance would be needed. Were there any newsworthy items from their group that they wanted to share, or recognition and accomplishments to brag about?

At the team meeting each assistant would bring their items forward and put the service areas on notice of the upcoming projects and needs. The service areas would take note of times they would be needed and could then report back to their team members so everyone would be aware and be prepared.

The team leaders from the service areas and the Office Manager would report to the team any new office procedures or software that was upcoming that we needed to be aware of.

After the meeting each Team Leader was then responsible for passing the minutes of the meeting to their team members. We were then more aware of what each of us was doing and someone who was having a down time could offer assistance where we knew the workload was heaviest.

Whether or not you have an opportunity to have team meetings, it is important to communicate with the service areas in your organization and it is always important to communicate with the assistants with whom you work the closest.

The importance of the buddy system in the workplace

I'm sure most of us will remember in elementary school going on field trips and being assigned a *buddy*. On those field trips we were responsible to keep track of our buddy and to look after each other. It is the same in the office. When we are working as a team we look after our team members. Here are some ways administrative assistants can work together as a team:

- Pay attention to what others in your team are doing. Can you pitch in and help when someone is swamped? It is always appreciated when someone can get a photocopying job done while another person sends a fax, giving us the needed time to complete an urgent transcription.
- If you need to take an unplanned day off your team members can help by:
  - o changing your Out-of-Office Assistant in your e-mail account.
  - o making sure your incoming mail, courier and faxes are looked after.
  - o offering assistance to the professional with whom you work. They will be very appreciative if someone lets them know they will be available to look after anything that needs to be done during your absence.

Always check with your team members and work out a strategy for covering for each other so you will be prepared when someone takes an unplanned day off.

Some organizations have the advantage of floater assistants to cover vacation periods, if your organization does not, then it will be important for the assistants to cover for each other while on planned days off as well.

The administrative assistant plays an important role in any organization and I believe any company that recognizes that will enjoy the benefits from staff who feel appreciated and acknowledged for the part they play in accomplishing the company's goals.

Chapter 3

Working in the Mailroom

A n e-mail comes around from the Mailroom staff, "Would the person who put an unaddressed envelope in the outgoing mail please let us know who this should be addressed to?"

Working in a service area of an organization can be a challenge, but in particular in the Mailroom. We try to courier packages to post office boxes. We leave incomplete instructions on the photocopy request forms and then wonder why it was done wrong. We put our registered mail in with the regular mail and then are upset because it didn't get registered. If a courier package doesn't make it to its destination, we are quick to make the Mailroom staff feel that it is somehow their fault. But most importantly, when we need something done we need it done NOW. How can the assistant and the Mailroom staff work more effectively together?

Communicate

If you know of a big photocopying job that you will need done, let your Mailroom staff know so they can prepare for it and adjust their schedules to accommodate your requests.

Is it really that urgent?

Be honest. Do you really need that job done in the next 30 minutes? Be realistic in your expectations. Is there a possibility you have the time to do the job yourself? It may be quicker and less stressful for everyone to do it yourself if you see the Mailroom staff is particularly busy.

Who took the last yellow sticky?

If you take the last item in the supply area of your Mailroom or notice that there are only a few items left, let someone know so more can be ordered.

It has to go out when?

If you are working on an urgent document that needs to be couriered out and it is getting close to the end of the day, make the Mailroom staff aware so that they know that you will be rushing in with your courier package at the last minute. A good suggestion would be to give them the address or addresses so they can prepare the courier slips ahead of time. They will appreciate it.

The busiest time in the Mailroom can be at the end of the day when all the courier companies are arriving for their last pick up, and the assistants are all arriving wanting to get their packages in the last courier run.

We are a team

Working together as a team will make our work lives easier. If you are fortunate enough in your organization to have team meetings, invite a member of the Mailroom staff to participate. Communicate to them any big jobs that are coming up or problems that need resolution. Having your Mailroom prepared ahead of time with this information will make everyone's job less stressful.

The Mailroom is the final checkpoint before a document leaves your organization. Appreciate that. They can pick up on errors before the envelope leaves the door.

Bottom line

Communicate with each other. Show respect for each other. Assist when necessary. Appreciate each other's deadlines and schedules and realize we are all working towards a common goal to do the best job possible.

TIME OUT

Need not apply

I informed the mailroom staff I was going to apply for a job with them. They said that I need not apply.

Were they saying I was not qualified? Actually, I know I would be horrible at the job and obviously they know it too. Collating, copying, binding, stacking and couriering is not my thing.

It takes all kinds of skills and people to run an office efficiently and having someone who can do a job well and be suited to it is a good match.

I asked them if what they were trying to say was that they didn't mind me visiting, but wouldn't want me to live there. After a chorus of yeses I got the point.

Chapter 4

Why Doesn't the IT Person Believe Me?

*H*ave you ever noticed when you are trying to explain a computer problem to an IT person they tend to look at you as if they don't quite believe what you are saying? IT people seem to speak a different language than I do. They are looking at it from a hardware point of view and I am looking at it from a software user point of view and sometimes we just don't understand each other.

Please tell me the answer is not always reinstall

Sometimes I am almost afraid to call for help as I don't know if I can handle another re-install. Take the time to discuss the problem with the IT person and see if they can come up with other solutions to fix the problem.

Can we communicate better with the IT Department?

We have to recognize they are the experts in what they do and I have no doubt they know their hardware programs inside and out as that is their expertise. Communication fails when they don't realize that we as the users know the software programs and what we want them to do. I have found that some of the best IT people are those who were former assistants and users of these programs. They understand what we are trying to accomplish, not just why the computer isn't working.

I was speaking to my brother about this and he had a good analogy. My brother is a great guitar player and has been playing since he was six years old. He told me he met a man who was an expert guitar craftsman who built guitars for a living. He knew everything there was to know about a guitar. The only thing he didn't know was how to play it. In order to know if his craftsmanship was successful he needed someone to play his guitar and when he heard it being played by someone who knew what they were doing they both could appreciate that guitar better.

I think the same applies with the IT people and the end users. There needs to be communication and understanding on both sides. IT are the computer experts, but we are the users and we both know what we are doing. We need to respect each other's expertise.

We are on the same team

The IT Department are a service department and are there to keep the systems working and to assist us when we don't know how to do something or to get our computers up and running again when they crash. An IT person once reminded me, and I know it's true, we are so used to getting things done in seconds that we get frustrated when the system slows down to minutes. I come from the time of the manual typewriter so I of all people should understand that when the computer slows down it is still faster than it used to be. Maybe some perspective would help. We have come a long way in technological advances. Communication on both sides will help us have a better working relationship with this very important and needed service area.

Chapter 5

The Floater Assistant

We all take holidays and when we are gone someone needs to fill in for us. One of my pet peeves when I come back from holidays is that nothing looks the same as before I left. My toolbars look different, my Outlook has changed, documents are saved in a way I would never think to find them again and where is my filing?

I thought putting together a few Do's and Don'ts for both the assistant and the floater assistant would help.

Do's and Don'ts

Do meet with the floater assistant before you leave on vacation.

Do fill out a form for your replacement with any information they might need: computer passwords and any upcoming tasks they will have to handle in your absence.

Don't change the computer settings or the workspace of the assistant you are replacing. If you must change the settings, take a PrintScreen of the settings and restore it back to the original settings before you leave that assignment.

If you are using the assistant's Outlook, *do* change the signature line to indicate you are sending the e-mail on their behalf.

Do put your initials on correspondence you type.

Do as much filing as you can if you've been asked to do so. If you are unsure about some filing, leave it in a folder for the assistant to do on their return.

Do leave a short note or e-mail for the returning assistant to give a summary of what you did while they were away and if there is anything that needs attention on their return.

If you are appreciative of the work the floater assistant has done for you in your absence, **do** send a thank you e-mail (I always copy the HR Manager as well). I think a job well done needs to be acknowledged and recognized.

We cannot expect the floater to do our job *exactly* the way we do it, but we can expect it to be done in a professional manner with the information we provide to them.

Chapter 6
The Challenges of Working for More Than One Person

I had always worked one on one, but in my new job I was going to be working for two very busy lawyers. I realized quite early on that I would have to make adjustments in my working style because of the many challenges of working for more than one person.

Here are some things I have learned as I have transitioned into this new role that I think would apply to anyone working for multiple bosses.

When I am given work by either of my bosses I have had to get into the habit of asking them when they need their task completed. I can then prioritize my workload and organize my day better. Sometimes I find it is a learning experience for your bosses as well, and it is nice if you can take the lead in making things run smoothly. Now when I ask them when they need it, unless it is extremely urgent, they usually ask me what is on my plate and then they make their decision based on that.

I organize my desk in such a way that I can accommodate both their needs. I have incoming mail trays for each of them and separate places for their filing, but otherwise I use my other trays for both of them. (See Part II - Chapter 8 - *Getting Organized and Staying that Way*)

All incoming work I put in order of priority and go through the pile as quickly as I can.

I maintain both of their calendars and print out a copy of each of their schedules for the day so I have something in front of me to refer to. I try to keep up to date on what their week is going to be like so I am aware of what may be coming up that they will need assistance on.

I also open and read their incoming mail and mark down any dates or deadlines and mark it in their calendars and in my Outlook Tasks, with reminders set, which helps me to plan and prioritize.

I have, on rare occasions, had to ask them to decide which job gets done first because I did not have time to meet both their deadlines. I find if they are aware of my workload they will try to work with me on priorities.

Fortunately, the assistants in my office work as a team and sometimes it is a simple matter of asking one of them to pitch in and help and between us we can meet the deadlines.

I actually now enjoy working for two people as it gives me variety in my day and I am learning to work with two individuals with different working styles. As long as you keep yourself and your desk organized it is not an impossible task.

* *

TIME OUT

The blame game

I was speaking to a friend and she jokingly said the office slogan for the assistant should be, "Stick around, I may need someone to blame." We laughed but sometimes it's true. People need to blame someone when something goes wrong and sometimes it is the assistant who gets blamed. The assistant then needs to blame someone so she blames the Mailroom staff and the Mailroom staff need to blame someone so they blame the courier company and on and on it goes playing the Blame Game.

PART V – MEETING PLACES

Chapter 1

Making Travel Arrangements: Are We There Yet?

aking travel arrangements for your boss can sometimes be stressful. It is important to ask the right questions to get them where they want to go.

I recall making travel arrangements for my boss who was travelling to New York City for a meeting. I was not aware there were three main airports he could fly to: JFK, LaGuardia and Newark International Airport. I had him flying into LaGuardia but his hotel room and meeting were right across town closer to another airport. Oops!

To avoid these types of situations, here are some questions you can ask your boss when making their travel arrangements:

- What kind of travel: Air, Train, Car?
- The day and time preferred for departure and return.
- If travelling by air do they have a preference as to where they are seated, window or aisle?
- Is there an airport they would prefer flying to and a hotel they would like to stay in?
- Do they need a rental car and, if so, what type of car do they want?
- If travelling by car do they require a map for directions and will they be claiming mileage? (I use MapQuest for directions and mileage).
- Is the business travel being charged to the company or to a client?

- Are they travelling with a business contact and want to sit next to them?
- Do they require a hotel room, restaurant reservation or a meeting room? Always remember to get confirmation numbers when you book anything.
- If they require a hotel room, what are their room requirements? (Smoking/Non-Smoking, King or Queen-sized bed.)
- If they are going to a conference, do they need to be registered? You are often able to book them a room in the hotel where the conference is being held.

I have found it more convenient and time saving to use a travel agency to make travel arrangements.

The advantages I have found in using a travel agency are:

- The service fee is minimal.
- It saves time. All you need to do is send them an e-mail with details and they do all the work.
- It is cost effective. The travel agent will do the work to get you the best deals possible.
- They ask the right questions to get you where you want to go.

Depending on how busy you are and your office policy, you can decide whether you prefer to book it yourself or use a travel agency.

Tip:

Be sure to check your travel tickets whether you get them by mail or by e-mail. From personal experience I have learned to check to see that the passenger name and the date and time on the ticket is correct. A travel agent we dealt with must have been having a bad day and put her name in the passenger section and my boss's name in the travel agent section. I received an urgent call from my boss at the airport saying he was having a hard time getting on the flight and could I fix it *immediately*.

Chapter 2

Organizing a Conference

Organizing a conference can be fun. Really! I enjoy it. The only problem is, you usually have to organize the conference and still do all your other work and that makes for some pretty hectic days leading up to the event. You definitely need to be organized.

Start with a good to-do list. I have included a sample to-do list at the end of this chapter. If you have never organized a large event, this should help get you started. I am convinced that with a good to-do list you can organize just about anything.

In my early years of being a secretary, I didn't want to have anything to do with organizing a conference or any event. Everything seemed to go wrong when I did. I organized a departmental group meeting once and when we got to the hotel they had no record of my reservation. Fortunately they were able to accommodate us, but I had the feeling I was jinxed when it came to organizing things like this.

Now I love the planning, organizing and especially the interaction with the people who attend. The day of the event is great as you get to meet the people you have only met by e-mail. As you are handing out name tags you can finally put a name to a face and greet them on behalf of your organization. It is nice to see all your hard work coming together and everything going smoothly. Of course you are madly scrambling behind the scenes to keep it that way.

Each time I organize an event I learn something. One dinner event I organized I must have been having a chocolate craving when I arranged the menu items. After a great meal the dessert was served – a rich chocolate cake. Break time comes around and I look and there are chocolate chip cookies and chocolate crunch bars. Then the next break comes around and -- more chocolate. Now when I set up menu items I get the help of the hotel event co-coordinator. They are a great resource to assist you in choosing meal items, suggesting table set up and just about anything to do with your event. They want to assist you to make it successful. I now have them on speed dial whenever I am organizing anything.

I am always preparing for the next event, so if something about this conference didn't go as nicely as I would have liked, I make a note of it on my to-do list to remind myself for the next time. You can be sure that I put NO CHOCOLATE on the to-do list under meal planning after the last event.

If you have materials that need to be printed for your conference, get a good printing company and realize they are the experts. Tell them what you need and they will let you know how you can accomplish that goal. When choosing a printing company keep your budget in mind and shop around for the best price and quality.

I put even the smallest things on my to-do list. You think you will re-member, but you are so busy on the day of the event that unless you have it written down you may forget.

Sample to-do list

Name of Event:
Date/Time of Event:
Location:

TASK	DUE DATE	RESPONSIBLE PERSON(S)	DONE

+ Finalize program topics and speakers.
+ Fix date and book location.
+ Arrange for food and audiovisual requirements.
+ Arrange set up of room and table(s) for registration.
+ Prepare invitation list.
+ Arrange for any promotional materials for the conference.
+ Arrange for PowerPoint (PPT) presentations and handouts. *Tip:* For the materials, instead of handing out hardcopies, try saving them

as a PDF document to be burned onto a CD (less expensive and environmentally friendly).

+ Arrange for printing and binding of materials if needed.
+ Prepare name tags for everyone attending, including your own organization's people who will be at the event (first name, last name, company name).
+ Advertise event.
+ Choose your contact person to receive registration requests and questions by e-mail or phone.
+ Keep a record of all registrants with their phone numbers and e-mail addresses.
+ If possible, prior to the event send a reminder to all registrants to confirm their registration.
+ Deliver materials to the venue.

The day of the conference:

+ Bring enough pens and pads for tables, unless you have arranged with the venue to supply them.
+ Bring any promotional materials you want to hand out.
+ Bring name tags and registration list (put in alphabetical order by last name on the registration table).
+ Bring pens, scissors, black marker, highlighter and extra blank name tags and name tag holders for the registration table.
+ Either arrange for signage with venue or bring your own signage to direct registrants to your event.
+ A checklist is a necessity to make sure everything you need is in the box going with you to the conference.

Chapter 3

Scheduling Meetings

Scheduling meetings can involve a lot of back and forth e-mailing and phone calls before you finally come up with a date and time when all your participants can be available. It is important to keep a good record of times and dates people have indicated they are available if you are the lead person in the scheduling.

A friend of mine gave me a good tip for scheduling meetings. She creates a table and uses it each time she has to schedule something. It is very easy to use and keeps everything neat and you can see at a glance where you are at with the scheduling.

Set up a table with five columns across, four rows down (or however many people are participating in the meeting). In the columns across put the available dates and times and in the rows down, put the names of the participants. As you phone or e-mail participants and find out their availability, put checkmarks or a Yes/No if they are available in the row beside their name and under the date and time that applies. You can customize the form according to your needs. I have included a sample on the next page.

When you hear from participants either by e-mail or phone, print out a copy of the e-mail or jot down the result of a phone call on a piece of paper and keep all this back-up information behind the meeting scheduling form as a quick reference.

Once the meeting is arranged, keep a copy of the meeting scheduling information in a file until the meeting is over in case you need to refer back to it.

MEETING NAME

List of Participants	Available Date/Time	Available Date/Time	Available Date/Time	MEETING REQUEST SENT
1st Person's name	X	X	✔	
2nd Person's name	✔	✔	✔	
3rd Person's name	✔	✔	✔	

Checklist *(do you need to do the following?)*:

* Confirm date, time and location
* Book room
* Reserve A/V equipment (laptop, LCD projector)
* Book teleconference line, polycom, videoconferencing equipment
* Order catering

"The meeting table I use is quite simple, but helps keep track of when participants are available. I think it's a good idea to give the participants a limited number of options: three or four dates are usually enough to choose from."

Denise Bellfoy, Executive Assistant

Calendar meeting tip

Your boss has a teleconference scheduled but is out of the office and will be joining the call on a wireless hand-held phone. An e-mail was sent with items the client wanted to discuss. In order for your boss to have all the information they need for the call, drag and drop the e-mail into the calendar meeting date. They can then view the information they need from their *wireless* before the meeting.

If you include an e-mail or comments in the meeting date I always recommend typing (SEE BELOW) or (OPEN TO READ COMMENTS) in either the Subject or Location box. If your boss is not in the habit of opening the meeting date he or she may not realize it is in there.

Other things you can put in the Comments section would be:

- call-in numbers if it is a teleconference
- agenda
- address and directions to get to the meeting
- confirmed attendance list with phone numbers (especially if your boss is the chair)
- and any other information you think would be helpful

Outlook tip to help with scheduling meetings

Here is a good tip if someone calls you wanting to check your boss's availability on multiple dates in the next month or so. Instead of going to each date one at a time you can view them all at once. Here's how:

1. Go to your calendar *Day* view.

2. Hold down the Ctrl key, and select your dates from the *small* calendar (the one that shows the full month). Click on the dates you want to look at, i.e. January 5, 9, February 5, 7. (To go to the next month, continue to hold down the Ctrl key and click on the arrow that brings you to the next month). If you are checking consecutive dates all in one week...hold down the Shift key and click on the first date and then click on the last date. For example February 1 and February 4, you will then see February 1-4.

3. You will now be able to see all the dates at a glance and know what your boss has scheduled for each of the days.

Note: You can use the Outlook Scheduling tool to set up meetings, but this only works if everyone keeps their calendars up to date.

Scheduling tip

To save time and numerous e-mails, a good tip for scheduling a meeting would be to have a conference call with all the assistants involved to come up with a date that works for everyone.

TIME OUT

Free food, or is it?

A friend was telling me when they have food brought in for meetings they almost need an armed guard to watch it. Once they left a food cart in the hall right outside the meeting room. The food was to be brought in after the presentation. The mayor was in attendance as well as the media and local celebrities. The chairman announced at the end of the presentation that refreshments and goodies were available just outside the door. When they went to get it from the hallway the trays had been picked clean.

Just because there is food on a tray doesn't mean it is meant for you. Always ask before helping yourself. As in my friend's example, it could be embarrassing to your organization.

Chapter 4

The Art of Minute Taking

*M*inute taking is an art! Anyone who is good at it is to be commended.

I have never had to take minutes, but I *almost* did many years ago. My boss came to my desk and told me he needed me to take minutes for a meeting. I had not been aware of the meeting and wasn't prepared. I started to sweat and my heart started pumping as I mumbled something about it being a long time since I had taken minutes and he had better tell me when I needed to write something down. As my boss and I entered the meeting room I heard, "Surprise!" Instead of a meeting it was a surprise baby shower for me. Whew! I had escaped having to take minutes once again.

Is the thought of taking minutes really that frightening? I thought so and I know others who feel the same way. I recently spoke to a friend who is a minute taker. She passed along her wisdom and experience and I noticed when we broke the steps down, it really didn't seem that daunting. I think that even I could do it.

Of course these tips are general ones and some meetings require more specific preparation, but they should be a help and a guide to you.

What you need to do before the meeting

Whether you are booking a meeting room on or off-site you need to ensure you have the space booked for the time and date you need it. If you require videoconferencing or teleconferencing, you will have to arrange that. An LCD projector, laptop and a screen will need to be available if there is going to be a presentation at the meeting. You will want to order food if required.

An agenda should be sent to the attendees with the previous minutes and all background documents. It is advisable to bring extra copies of the agenda and attachments to the meeting in case someone arrives without theirs.

Rather than sending the agenda and attachments in hardcopy form, a preferable way would be by e-mail or some offices and boards now have a website where they post the agenda and any back-up materials, which can then be retrieved by the meeting attendees or board members when they log onto the site.

Getting yourself prepared

In order to be as prepared as possible for the meeting you should look at the attendance sheet from the past minutes to know who is on the committee and will be attending. If this is the first time you are taking minutes at this particular meeting, read through three or four previous meeting minutes to familiarize yourself with the issues.

You can also start to create an agenda from the last minutes and present it for approval by the chair of the meeting. Once the agenda is approved you can use the new agenda to start the minutes.

If you start the minute template ahead of time and fill in as much information as possible, you will be better prepared going into the meeting.

The first thing you need to do in the meeting is to take attendance. You are required to record those who are present, anyone who sent their regrets, any guests, and remember to record your name as the recorder or minute taker.

If you don't know all the people in the room ask them to introduce themselves, or make sure there are nameplates provided. Minute takers should not be afraid to speak up and ask people to identify themselves for the minutes, especially those calling in or on videoconference who may forget to identify themselves before speaking. If the participants do not speak clearly you need to ask them to repeat what they said for the minutes.

The two most important people in a meeting are the chair and the minute taker. Your job is important.

A good way to record the minutes is on a laptop. You have already started your minutes with as much information as you have been able to gather ahead of time so you are as prepared at this point as you can be.

When you are recording the minutes you should record each item in the same order as the agenda lists them, not in the order they talk about them.

If the chair says this is not for the minutes you need to take your hands off the keyboard so the meeting participants know it is not being recorded.

Don't feel offended if you are asked to leave a meeting during an *in-camera session*. For example, if they are discussing staff or executive salaries they will ask staff to leave. No minutes are taken during an in-camera session, but you still have a role to play as you will need to record for the minutes the duration of the in-camera session. Be aware of the time you left the meeting and the time you go back in.

The chairperson can make the difference

Denise Bellfoy an Executive Assistant and regular minute taker says, "A *good chairperson can make your job much easier.*"

A good chair will keep the meeting on time and will summarize the discussion for the minute taker. If the chair is sensitive to a long meeting he or she can call a break. Sometimes the hardest part for the minute taker is to stay alert and concentrate, especially if the meeting is long and drawn out.

If there are motions for approval, a good chair will word the motion for the minutes.

Some things to be aware of

If there is a presentation in the meeting, you do not need to record the presentation in the minutes, but you will need to include a copy of the presentation with the minutes when you send them out.

Some good advice for the minute taker would be to sit to the left of the chair and take as much space as you need. Important people take a lot of room and you want to be as comfortable as possible and have everything easily accessible to you.

When transcribing minutes avoid writing "he said, she said." Summarize the conversations and record the outcome. Again, if you have a good chair, he or she will be able to guide you on what to record.

Avoid using emotional words when recording the minutes. Use business words. For example, do not use "she felt," but rather "the committee member agreed."

It is recommended you do a rough draft of the minutes within two hours after the meeting with a final draft within 24 hours. The chair will need to review and approve the minutes before they are finalized and sent out.

Here are a few examples of different types of meetings:

Operational meetings

An operational meeting is a meeting that deals with the business of an organization. A table format is the easiest form to take minutes at an operational meeting.

I would recommend setting up a table something like this:

Agenda Item	Discussion	Responsible Person	Timeline

Items from the operational meeting will then be brought forward for board approval.

Board meetings

A board meeting is normally run by *Roberts Rules of Order*, which is a recognized guide on how to run a meeting. A board can also set their own rules if they choose.

Items requiring approval by the board are summarized by the chair and the minute taker will need to record the motion, who *moved* the motion for approval and who *seconded* it and whether or not the motion was passed by the board.

There should be an Appendix of Action Items attached to your minutes (which is basically a to-do list).

It is important to note that board minutes are public once they are approved.

Meeting adjourned

Now that wasn't so bad was it? I found when the steps needed to record the minutes were set out, it made the task seem less overwhelming. Minute taking is not easy, but if you go in prepared it can be accomplished without fear and trembling each time you are called upon to take minutes.

Chapter 5

How Important is it to Keep an Accurate Contact List?

As I collected my mail I noticed that one of the letters in my mailbox was addressed to my brother who lives in the same building as I do. The envelope was addressed to Mr. and Mrs, but my brother is not married. I called my brother and told him about the letter and he asked me to open it for him to let him know what it was. When I opened it I was shocked to read, "I would like to extend my sympathy to you on the loss of a loved one...." We did not have a recent death in our family.

I read on, "Would I be able to offer my assistance to you at this time in the choosing of a memorial stone?"

Aside from the fact that this marketing letter was in *very* poor taste, this definitely was an example of someone not keeping accurate contact information.

Think about this in regard to your office. You are doing a mass mailing, sending invitations for a conference or seminar, or you are sending sales brochures or company information, hoping to get new business and you address it to a CEO who was fired from that company, or to the President, but you have spelled his name wrong, or the company has changed their name or address. There can be a number of reasons for a change, including the recipient has passed away, but if the recipient passed away five years ago and you are still sending things to that address, somebody is not keeping their records up to date.

In many cases, especially when a company is moving or changing their name, they will send notices advising of the change of information. When you get these notices make sure you change your contact cards and notify anyone else in your company who might need to know about this change of information. For example, your Accounting Department and your Marketing Department if you have one.

Sometimes a mistake like this can mean loss of business for your company. In my example, you can be sure I will not be going to this company if I ever need to purchase a memorial stone. This error has left a bad impression of what might be a perfectly good company, who made a bad marketing decision and didn't have the correct contact information.

* *

TIME OUT

Ladies first!

I have noticed that most young female executives and assistants are not too keen on the ladies first order of things. I pointed out to one of my co-workers recently that I think it makes for order when boarding and getting off an elevator or entering boardrooms or offices.

I appreciate it especially when there is a group of people gathered at the elevator waiting for the one door to open. It is nice to allow the ladies to enter first and then the men enter. There is the odd time a man will go ahead of everyone and not respect that order and I find that annoying as it disrupts what was an orderly flow. Maybe we need a better etiquette so it won't be a male/female thing, but for now it works.

Who goes first?

We were joking at the office about elevator etiquette and who should go first. One person suggested that the tallest should go first. This person is over 6 feet.

Someone else suggested it should be the oldest who goes first. I laughed and said, "Then nobody would want to get on the elevator." I would say, "You go first." Then the next person would say, "No, I insist, you go first." Nobody would want to go first and admit they were the oldest.

PART VI – OFFICE CONVERSATIONS

Chapter 1

If you don't want your boss to know about it, that is a good indication that you shouldn't write about it on your blog.

Blogging, Social Networking and Work: Do They Mix?

We live in a day and age when we can go on the Internet and open a profile on a social networking site or create a blog or even post a comment on a site that puts our name and, if we choose, our photo out there. There is no cost and it is relatively easy to do, but is it always in our best interest to do so and can it have a negative impact on our career?

What some people are writing

On an interactive forum for administrative assistants someone wrote that they had posted a comment on another site, including posting their photo, and had made a negative comment about their boss. The person felt bad about it and was worried that this was going to affect their employment. They had a valid concern.

On another social site someone named the company that they worked for and had written very specific information about some internal things that were going on in their organization.

Can what you write in a public forum get you fired?

If you do a quick search on the Internet and type in *blogging can get you fired*, you will get many hits with articles about cases where people had blogged about their employer and it caused them problems at work and in some cases got them fired. There is even an article about children who wrote negative posts about their parents on social networking sites that affected their parent's employment.[18]

If you are a blogger or are on social networking sites it would be worth it to check out these articles. You need to be very careful what you write in a public forum. Anybody, including your employer, can and does read them.

Some common sense rules for blogging and social networking

If you are on a public forum you should never write about specific incidents at work, but be very general.

Never name anyone from work on a blog or on a social networking site without their express written permission and, even if you do have their permission, carefully consider whether it is in everyone's best interest to post it.

Unless you are a contributor to a corporate blog, it is probably a good idea not to name your employer on your blog or social networking site.

Never plagiarize someone else's writing, but give proper acknowledgement and citations when using other people's work, including getting permission to quote them.

Not everything that is written on the Internet is true. Before quoting something you have seen on the Internet, check out the source to make sure it is a reliable site. You can avoid embarrassment and lack of credibility by verifying your information, especially if you are using your blog to showcase your skills and expertise.

Never write when you are angry, including posting comments on other people's blogs and interactive forums as it can come back to haunt you.

It is a good idea to put a disclaimer on your blog that the opinions expressed are those of the author only. There are other things that you also need to consider writing in your disclaimer to protect yourself and if you

---

18 Diamant, Aaron, *Parent Trap*, http://www.todaystmj4.com/features/ony-ourside/10723141.html, (accessed December 26, 2007

simply do an Internet search and type in *writing a blog disclaimer* you will get lots of useful information to help you.

What happens in Vegas stays in Vegas

Not so with the Internet. Be careful what you post about your personal life. Be aware that if you have taken a sick day and then blog about the fun time you had at the party you went to, your blogging audience can be anybody who happens to click on your site. The same applies to social networking sites. Think about what you write in your Status line. If you put *hungover* on that same day you took off sick and it is read by your employer that would not reflect well on you.

Can blogging be good for your career?

Social networking can be fun and used properly can be a great tool to market yourself. It is not all bad news.

It seems everybody is doing it. Have you noticed when you go on a corporate website there is often a link to their blog. Corporations are setting up blogs as a link to their websites to showcase their company on a more human level and depending on the content of the blog can make their website a very popular place to be -- which is good for business.

Blogging has become so popular that politicians and governments are also getting in on the action.

What about us?

Can setting up a blog site to market our skills be viewed as a positive marketing tool by a potential employer?

Blogging can create many opportunities to advance your career. Employers do check the Internet when they are interviewing potential candidates, therefore, having a well-written blog with knowledge sharing about your specific area of expertise can showcase your skills. An employer can get a good idea of your style and personality by the things you have written.

To write articles on your blog you will need to do research on many subjects in your field and as a result you will become more expert at what you do. It will test your knowledge and skills and may sometimes change the way you do things to be more effective in your job.

You will be amazed when you notice the number of visitors you have had on your blog, even visitors from different parts of the world. People are watching and reading.

Enjoy the social side of the Internet, but be careful and don't get so comfortable that you let your guard down. Educate yourself on what you can and cannot do and blog smart.

* * * * * * * * * * * * * * * *

TIME OUT

I work in a law firm so I am fully aware that blogging can get you fired and I try to blog smart. I tell people I am probably the only blogger who can truly say "My lawyers are looking into it," because they actually are.

* * * * * * * * * * * * * * * * * *

After posting a few of my articles twice in the same month, I decided to write this on my blog for my Thought for the Day. "Old bloggers never die, we just start repeating our posts."

Chapter 2

You May Feel Like it, But Don't!

s an assistant I have always been amazed when someone has called me wanting to speak to my boss and then has been rude on the phone. The administrative assistant can often be the professional gatekeeper as to who gets in to see the boss and how quickly they get to speak to them on the phone. I would not recommend using your position to make things difficult for someone trying to reach your professional, but it has never made sense to me when people have done that. So how should you handle the situation?

+ Be professional. Speak calmly to the person and do the best you can to reassure them that you will give their name and number to your boss.
+ Don't take it personally. I would give the person the benefit of the doubt and assume that they normally would not behave like that. They are probably under a lot of stress due to a deadline or a situation that may have happened and they are taking that stress out on you.
+ Ask if you can refer them to someone else in the office who may be able to help them.
+ Don't argue.
+ If you were unable to resolve the situation, tell your boss. Don't keep this information to yourself. Tell your professional and let him or her handle it.

Chapter 3

Working Remotely From Home

*I*n today's electronic age it is becoming easier to work from home. You can log on to your computer at home and have access to everything you would have at the office. With the wireless hand-held device you can get your e-mails, retrieve your phone messages and get work-related phone calls from home, on the road or from a beachfront hotel in the Bahamas.

Many professionals work from home on occasion, and I believe the assistant's role can be even more important as we are the contact for the professional and the client to keep things running smoothly at the office.

But can the assistant work from home? I have a few friends who are hooked up to work at home and do so when necessary. One person I know works full-time at home as an assistant, but in her case she runs the office of a volunteer organization and her home is the office base. All couriers are sent there and the business phone, fax and computer are all at her home.

She has a unique situation and I know she loves the freedom, but I also know she is very, very busy and still has to accomplish a lot in one day. She said the challenge she has is trying to get her family to understand she is at work. She also confessed that sometimes she wakes up at night thinking of something she needs to do and ends up going down to her office and doing some work in the wee hours of the morning.

Although the idea of working at home sounds appealing to me, I am not sure I would have the discipline to do it. I think I need the structure of the office environment to keep myself on track.

For those who may be interested in looking into working at home, I found an article entitled, "Working At Home? Five Things You Can't Be Without." [19]

Times are definitely changing and it will be interesting to see how the future unfolds for the business office and for the assistant.

---

19 Working At Home? Five Things You Can't Be Without, http://www.canadajobs.com/articles/viewarticle.cfm?ArticleID=1211 (accessed January 26, 2008)

Chapter 4
The Virtual Assistant: The Business of Working at Home

With the advances made in technology, the ability to set up a home virtual assistant business has become quite doable and in many cases, very profitable. There is technology to get voicemails and faxes in an e-mail format and transcriptions can be sent by e-mail as well. We can connect to the office computer and have access to everything you would have if you were in the office. With the addition of a business line you can easily re-direct business calls to your home and no one would know that they were calling someone's home and not the office.

The technology is available to set up a virtual office at home and work by contract for many different employers, and there are entrepreneurs doing just that.

The role of the virtual assistant can be limited to areas you want to work in, i.e. personal assistant and desktop publishing, or the sky is the limit with any number of functions you can fulfill for your client's business and personal needs. It all depends on your abilities and what you want to do. The work is out there and the Internet has provided the means to do the job effectively and without borders. Your employer can now be anywhere in the world with just a click of the mouse.

Two heads are better than one

Running a virtual business doesn't mean you have to do it all yourself. It is easy to virtually hire someone in another city or country to assist you. Your expertise may be in accounting, word processing and marketing, but you can easily partner with someone to do your web design and graphics work. You can also contract yourself out to virtual assistant firms to lend your expertise to their businesses all from the comfort of your home.

The virtual office

Your virtual office can be tucked away in the corner of your house or in a corner of your basement, but it does require state of the art technology and equipment to be able to meet the needs of your clients. Investing in good quality equipment is a must. If you are not a hardware person you will want to have a contract with an IT company who can assist you when you run into computer problems, especially if you are in the middle of a rush job for a client.

Purchasing an ergonomic workstation is also essential as you will spend hours sitting at your desk in front of your computer.

Networking in the virtual community

Becoming part of the virtual community is a necessity for the virtual assistant. Networking among assistants is necessary whether virtual or in an office building. Assistants depend on their co-workers to ask questions and get feedback, and it is the same for the virtual assistant. There are virtual office groups worldwide to share your successes and concerns with and to share your expertise. Having a network of assistants is key to a successful business.

The demands on executives have increased and the need for assistance is not going to go away. As corporations downsize and technology advances, the business of the virtual assistant will only increase and become more doable and profitable in the future.

Chapter 5

The 24/7 Executive:
Are Our Bosses Addicted?

With the use of the wireless hand-held device, our bosses now seem to be working continually. Is the ability to conduct business 24/7 the new high? How is that impacting the role of the assistant and can we help?

The wireless corporate addiction

A young lawyer puts his wireless hand-held device under his pillow so he won't miss that all-important call or e-mail. He doesn't want to miss the opportunity if someone should want to get in touch with him. Initially he is somewhat surprised when he is awakened in the wee hours of the morning with incoming messages, but now he considers it normal to receive e-mails at any time of the day or night.

A corporate executive is concerned that while on a cruise in a remote part of the world he will only be able to check his messages when he disembarks on land. His spouse endures patiently until the next port of call, while his assistant waits anxiously to see when he logs on so messages can be exchanged.

It is such a noticeable phenomenon that the name *Crackberry* has been coined for those who are addicted.

Some disturbing symptoms of this *wireless* addiction are feelings of anxiety when you are unable to go online or are out of service range, and neglecting real relationships for *wireless* ones.

Colleagues and assistants unknowingly become enablers as they feed this compulsion to check messages by taking advantage of their online availability. Employers may even fuel the addiction by their expectations of 24/7 accessibility.

The laptop started the excitement with the convenience of being able to bring your computer on the road. With the *wireless* we can now carry our computer in our pocket. We have gone from the fascination of the big screen to the addiction of the small screen and executives have taken to it with a passion.

The day the Berry went Black

April 17, 2007 will be remembered for when service was interrupted for hours, well into the next day, for millions of users of the wireless hand-held device in North America. Offices were buzzing about what could have happened. "Where were you when...?" or "How did you cope?" were the kinds of questions executives were asking each other. People held their collective breaths wondering when service might be restored and they could get back to thumbing their way through their messages.

Getting the cold thumb

If you have ever waited for the elevator or for public transit with one of these users you will have gotten the cold thumb. They do not acknowledge the people around them because their focus is entirely on their *wireless*.

Physiotherapists are seeing more repetitive strain injuries on hands and thumbs from this overuse, with the increase in tendonitis and carpal tunnel syndrome. Some users have had to withdraw and go cold turkey because of the damage.

Lighten up

Some websites have taken a light-hearted look at this pastime and are making suggestions for other uses for the *wireless* device, such as using the *wireless* as a night light to go to places it has never gone before – directing blurry eyed executives to the bathroom.

Paparazzi type sightings of *Crackberry* users have become the new frenzy and are posted on websites. Who will they spot using their *wireless*?

People are also coming up with new words to express their online addiction such as *blirting*, which is the equivalent of wireless flirting, and *talking with your thumbs* to explain the wireless chit chat.

Don't Berry and Drive, however, may be the new catch phrase to describe the emerging socially unacceptable behaviour of driving while on your *wireless*. The dangers of focusing on your *wireless* while driving are becoming a real concern, and rightly so. Concentrating on anything other than your driving is a danger to yourself and to others.

The changing role of the assistant

With the increasing demands on the time of the executive at work and at play, the stresses are mounting as their workloads are increasing, and they need the help of their assistants more and more.

It used to be when our bosses were away it was a time for the assistant to catch up on filing, take messages and pass on any urgent requests that needed to be handled in their absence. Now when our bosses are on the road, or on vacation, the need for assistance is becoming critical. No longer are people going through the assistant to contact the boss, they are going directly to the boss through the wireless hand-held device. As our bosses are waiting to connect to a flight or during a break in a meeting, they are e-mailing their assistants and asking them for the status on a file so they can report back to a client or management.

Some professionals, out of necessity, have given their assistant access to their Inbox so the assistant can screen messages and weed out what they do not need to look at or identify things that they can handle on their behalf.

It is becoming increasingly important for the assistant to read e-mails thoroughly to look for action items or dates that need to be put in their boss's calendar and handle requests for information.

The ability to be organized has taken on a whole new meaning for the assistant as we turn our attention to helping our professionals cope. Some assistants who have remote access to their work e-mail accounts at home have also taken to checking e-mails in the evenings and off hours to keep up with the demands.

The assistant can become a part of the solution, but a strategy between the executive and their assistant needs to be made to handle these types of issues.

This may well be the generation of the 24/7 workforce. Are we up for the challenge or do we need to step back and re-evaluate? It will be interesting to see how the role of the assistant will be impacted and changed as we move forward to this new way of doing business.

Chapter 6

Employee Assistance Programs: Taking the Fear Out of Asking for Help

E mployee Assistance Programs are a benefit offered by many employers to give employees and their family members easy access to professional counselling services. The primary purpose of the Employee Assistance Program (EAP) is to help employees solve problems that might be interfering with their work and personal lives.

EAPs have received the thumbs up by unions, management and business owners who recognize that helping employees at work and at home is of mutual benefit to their organizations.

I was first introduced to the EAP program when I came back to the workforce after taking some time off to raise my daughter. A co-worker told me that she was getting help for her son. Employers offer EAP to family members as well as employees as they are recognizing that when things are not right at home our performance at work can be affected.

It wasn't until many years later that I felt the need to ask for assistance. It was a stressful time in my life and I just needed someone to help me put things in perspective. The call was a hard one to make. I think we all have a hard time asking for help, but the person who took the call handled it with professionalism and compassion. I never felt uncomfortable and they were able to quickly assess and direct my enquiry to the appropriate counsellor.

I think sometimes in our busy lives we don't feel we even have the time to make the effort to get help. I was in that position and couldn't see how I would be able to fit the appointments into my busy schedule. I was told that I could have the counselling sessions over the telephone at the convenience of the counsellor and myself. That was such a help to me because I don't own a vehicle and getting places, especially in the evening, could be a stress in itself.

I was also given the option to request a male or female counsellor or someone of my ethnic background if that was a concern for me. If I wanted to speak to someone of my faith background, they would make every effort to accommodate me in this area as well.

Initially I felt uneasy about talking on the phone with a counsellor that I couldn't even see, but she was able to put me at ease right from the start. They encourage you to talk to them and they offer suggestions and evaluate what they think will help you. The duration of the session is up to you and your counsellor. If you decide you do not need further assistance you are not pressured to continue, but you are offered a toll-free number to call if you feel the need for follow up.

EAP and work

Our EAP provider sends us monthly newsletters with helpful tips for family and job-related issues. They are available to give on-site lunch 'n learn sessions to interested employees on a variety of topics including: Difficult Working Relationships, Coping with Grief, Eldercare and many other topics that are relevant to today's employees.

Your EAP is just a phone call away. Be assured that everything you say is held in the strictest confidence. Not even your employer will know you called. If you are feeling stressed due to work or home, investigate what help is available to you through your EAP or consult with your family physician.

Chapter 7

The Ergonomic Workstation: Health and Safety

I have experienced some of the downside of our profession from a health and safety perspective. That is most likely because I've been at it for almost 30 years.

Some examples of what can go wrong are eye strain, shoulder and neck problems, carpal tunnel syndrome, repetitive strain injuries, back problems and the list can go on.

It is very important for the younger assistants to use good practices now to avoid problems in the future.

Some things I have found to be important are:

+ Good posture at your work station.
+ Adjusting your chair to the proper height.
+ Setting your screen to the proper eye level.
+ Adjusting the glare on your computer.
+ Resting your forearms on something while mousing and typing.
+ Using an adjustable document holder for reading and typing.

These are just a few hints I received as a result of an ergonomic assessment of my workstation and they have improved my comfort level at work a great deal.

The Canadian Centre for Occupational Health and Safety's website has some helpful health and safety tips for office ergonomics.[20]

---

20 Canadian Centre for Occupational Health and Safety, http://www.ccohs. ca/oshanswers/ergonomics/office/ (accessed October 9, 2007)

Chapter 8

Non-Verbal Communication: Are We Being Heard?

I am sure we all remember our mothers telling us, "If you can't say anything nice, you shouldn't say anything at all." If you are a parent you have probably said the same thing to your own children. Can we communicate by saying nothing? I think we can and by not uttering a word we can be heard loud and clear.

For example, if you get a new haircut and nobody says anything about it, don't you get the impression that they don't care for it? People generally do not want to hurt anyone's feelings so if we don't like something we don't say anything at all.

I take the bus to work and I notice when a bus comes by that is not the one I am waiting for, the bus driver and I communicate without saying a word. I turn my face a bit and take a step back or look down. He looks at my non-verbal language and assumes I do not want that bus and continues along his route.

I think husbands and wives and people who have known each other a long time have probably experienced this on a deeper level. They get to know each other so well that they can communicate with a glance, a slight nod, a smile or even a glare.

What about at the office? Do we knowingly or unknowingly give non-verbal messages to our bosses and co-workers?

I remember at one job I was in, it was extremely busy and I would sigh when my boss brought me more work. It became a joke between us until my performance appraisal time and one of the questions was, "How do I handle my workload?" My boss had four options to choose from and yes, you guessed it, one of the options was "sighs loudly when given work." My sighing could have given my boss the impression that I didn't have time for more work and it wasn't welcomed. I haven't sighed since, but my boss and I laughed about that one for a long time.

I think we can communicate to our co-workers without saying a word by our smile or lack of it. A smile is welcoming and pleasant and people are drawn to you when you smile. By our smile, we show ourselves to be approachable and pleasant. Your boss will not feel he is burdening you with his requests. On the other hand we can greet those who dare come to our desk with a "What now?" look that leaves people with the impression that we do not want to be helpful and "Don't you dare ask."

Do you ever wonder if your boss is listening to you because of his non-verbal communication? His eyes may be on the computer screen or he is not giving you his full attention in other ways. Most business professionals are extremely busy and sometimes they are thinking of their next task or a problem that needs to be solved. This would not be the best time for you to sit down and ask for a raise.

Communication is important, whether at work or at home. We can communicate without saying a word and that may be speaking louder than our words. What are you saying?

* * * * * * * * * * * * * * * *

"We have two ears and one mouth so that we can listen twice as much as we speak."

EPICETETUS

"Snarling at other folks is not the best way of showing the superior quality of our own character."

CHARLES HADDON SPURGEON

Chapter 9

When You Go to the Bathroom With Your Boss: Same-Sex Working Relationships

T he U.S. Department of Labor's website, Women's Bureau, reports that in 2006 "women accounted for 51% of all workers in the high-paying management, professional and related occupations."[21] When you put that statistic together with the fact that the role of the administrative assistant is mainly dominated by women, with men only representing 5% of the workers,[22] the likelihood of working in a same-sex working relationship with a woman is increasing. If you are a woman from the baby boomer age it is also more likely that you will be working for a much younger woman.

---

21   U.S. Department of Labor, Quick Stats 2006, http://www.dol.gov/wb/stats/main.htm (Source: U.S. Department of Labor, Bureau of Labor Statistics, Employment and Earnings, 2006 Annual Averages and the Monthly Labor Review, November 2005) (accessed January 13, 2008). Canadian Statistics can be found at: Stats Canada, *Women in Canada*, http://www.statcan.ca/Daily/English/060307/d060307a.htm (accessed February 1, 2008)

22   Chicago Tribune, A job once filled by men became a pink profession (2006), http://goucher.edu/documents/MediaHits/Chicago%20Tribune%20news_%20A%20job%20once%20filled%20by%20men%20became%20a%20pink%20profession.pdf (accessed January 13, 2008)

Gone are the days when companies had executive bathrooms

I entered the workforce in 1974 and until recently had never worked for a woman and I didn't think I wanted to. I had heard all the horror stories from other assistants complaining about mood swings, high expectations, perfectionist tendencies and the list went on. I have found none of those things to be true however. I find working for a woman has been a refreshing change with the added bonus that she understands me.

She respects my knowledge and experience and looks to me for assistance and guidance in the areas where she knows I have expertise. I think the fact that I am close to her mother's age makes it harder for her to view herself as my boss, but rather she sees me as a co-worker.

Regardless of how she feels, she is my boss, the same as any man has ever been, and I am her employee. I respect the position she holds and look forward to seeing her advance in her career and cheer her on as she goes where women are just beginning to feel more at home.

It still surprises me however when we share the same bathroom space. I am not used to discussing work issues with my boss while fixing my hair or washing my hands at the sink. The bathroom was my private place to go where I would see my female co-workers and we could have a quick chat and complain if we had too. Not anymore. You never know if your boss is in the next stall!

* *

Do we really want to go there?

Today, there is even talk of men and women sharing the same bathroom space, as portrayed in a popular television series.

Same-sex working relationships and sharing bathroom space with my boss is one thing, but I hope I retire before I see unisex bathrooms in the office. There are some things that you just don't want members of the opposite sex to know about you, especially co-workers.

A friend of mine works in an office where men and women do share the same single bathroom and she compares it to the complaints mothers have long had at home with the bathroom habits of husbands and sons. It's a brave new world out there.

Chapter 10

Loyalty and Work

I noticed a co-worker putting on a hat with a competitor's logo on it and it made me think of loyalty in the workplace. How loyal are you to your company and your boss? If someone offered you a higher-paying job would you take it without a second look back or would you hesitate because you really like the company you work for and feel loyal to your boss?

Big Daddy is watching

It is hard to feel loyal to a big corporation. Management, and especially those in executive positions, may feel more loyal to their company because they are involved in the decision making and risks involved in running it. The success or failure of the company can depend on their loyalty to the cause. I doubt that staff would feel the same way about the companies they work for, although some companies have been successful in getting their staff on board in tooting the company horn.

Upper management seldom communicate company plans down the ranks and sometimes staff find out more about their company in the newspaper than they do by working there, which undermines company loyalty among staff.

Big corporations should take the time to educate their staff on who they are and what their goals are. Involving staff may help to make them more eager and loyal.

But I like my boss

I think where loyalty really comes into play for the assistant is our relationship with our boss. If we have a good working relationship, we tend to think twice before moving on to something else. A good working fit is sometimes the glue that makes you stick with a company.

When I enjoy working for someone, loyalty to that person and that job become even more important to me than salary. I am reluctant to leave if I am happy with my boss and job.

Loyalty to yourself and your career

Sometimes we need to make a change in our job and it has nothing to do with loyalty to your company or to your boss, but what is best for you and your career.

When I speak to assistants who are close to my age it seems we are from a generation that doesn't like to move on as much as the younger generation. Some of us stay in the same job from high school until retirement. We are firmly entrenched, but that is not always the best place to be.

The younger generation seem to be career minded and tend to move and change jobs more often. I think loyalty may have a different meaning for them. They are loyal while in their job, but don't mind moving somewhere else if it is a wise career move, if the salary and benefits are better or if there are more opportunities for advancement.

There is probably a good balance between these two perspectives. Employers like to have someone they can rely on to be there for awhile. It is expensive to train someone new and the position suffers from not having a full-time person dedicated to it. It is a good move by the employer to try and keep their staff happy. But it is also not good to stay in the same job year in and year out just for the stability. It is good for us at times to take the plunge and make a change that will benefit our careers and give us fresh challenges and new ideas on how to do things. We can get in a rut by sticking around too long.

Loyalty in a job is good and necessary, but if you have to move on you shouldn't feel you have let your employer down when a better opportunity comes along.

* * * * * * * * * * * * * *

"*Change is the essence of life. Be willing to surrender what you are for what you could become.*"

ANONYMOUS

Chapter 11

The Paperless Society: A Dream or a Necessity?

A woman in my office doesn't think it will be possible to have a paperless office, but I disagree. I think in the future we will see paperless as the norm, but we still have a long way to go. We have made impressive strides in that direction with the use of e-mail, word processing, document management programs, e-filing and the ability to scan documents.

Online e-magazines, blogs and feeds are now readily available to pass on information, and I have seen the early stages of online books that you can take with you just as you would a paper book.

Many of us have already become paper free when it comes to having our paycheques automatically deposited, doing our banking and making bill payments online. We are getting there, but the problem may not be with the technology, but in our willingness to share in the solution.

When did paper become a bad word?

I remember as a young secretary in the late 70's being concerned about the paper waste I saw in my office and even then having a conscience about it and wondering if there was some way that we could re-use it. It wasn't something people talked about back then. We have come a long way as a society in understanding the need to manage waste.

I think my generation's answer was recycling. Today's generation, how-ever, wants more than just recycling. They want to be good stewards of our earth in all areas of waste and after so many years of mismanagement, they have a valid reason for wanting to do so.

Public pressure has made governments move to set new targets and goals for the environment, and they have made advances in going paperless with the acceptance of e-filing of documents. We need to go even further, however, if we are going to realize the possibility of a paperless society.

What kind of global footprint are you leaving?

The new buzz words when it comes to the environment are environ-mental sustainability and carbon footprints.

Environmental sustainability is the vision that what we do today must not affect the quality of life for tomorrow. This involves governments, corporations and ordinary citizens who care about what we will leave to future generations.

A carbon footprint is a measurement of the amount of green house gases that I produce in my own little space by the choices I make in what products and services I use or the form of transportation I take and many other areas. The ability to reduce my footprint makes it even more per-sonal for me to be a better steward.

New rules

As more and more people jump on the paperless bandwagon, they are insisting on eliminating the need for paper and we are beginning to listen. Materials that used to be handed out at conferences and in schools are now made available on CDs or posted on websites for easy access. In a paperless world the need to have a computer or have access to one will be a must.

As e-mail becomes the preferred choice in business correspondence, e-mail management will become even more important and necessary. There is software already available to save e-mails directly into our document management systems. E-mail etiquette rules will also be essential to follow and will become the new standard for business writing.

New problems

In a paperless society there will be a need for greater security to increase people's comfort levels in using the technology and therefore eliminating the need for paper. Financial institutions are already encouraging customers to access their bank statements online and reassuring us that their sites are secure. All these advances will however come with a cost that will undoubtedly be passed on to the consumer.

With the increased use of electronic devices, proper ergonomics will become a factor with the need for better workstations and decreased glare on computer screens. Office workers and young people especially will be affected by this.

In schools the computer has become the new notebook. Children are on some sort of electronic device a good part of the day. We will need to learn the proper way to use our technology to avoid injuries.

With all our technological advances and knowledge, we will not go paperless until people learn that they do not have to press *Print*, and I believe they will only do that as their trust increases in the technology, laws change to accept e-filing of all documents and more people speak out about the importance to our environment.

It will be interesting to see how this next generation meets the challenges as we march on to the goal of being a truly paperless society.

Chapter 12

Being Green in the Office

*H*ow can we be better stewards of our environment at the office? My sister and I have come up with a few ideas with the assistance of her daughter, and my niece, Angela Crosbie, an environmentally-aware university student:

+ Take a bus to work, walk, bicycle or carpool if possible.
+ Photocopy or print double sided (post a sign by the photocopier if you need to).
+ Do you really need to print it? Burning it on a CD might work just as well.
+ Recycle paper from the printer areas (be careful not to recycle confidential waste: either shred it or put it in secure bins - see Part II - Chapter 10 – *To Shred or Not to Shred: Disposing of Confidential Documents*).
+ Ensure your office has plenty of recycle bins by each desk - as well as large recycle bins for cans, glass, newspapers and mixed waste paper.
+ Recycle your kitchen office garbage.
+ E-mail telephone messages to save on paper clutter and waste.
+ E-cycle: participate in recycling used electronic office equipment.
+ If you are in a position to do so, order recycled paper for your office. If not, talk to your boss about the possibility of ordering it.
+ Take your lunch to work in recyclable containers.
+ Use a *real cup* for coffee (or drinks) and avoid using *polystyrene foam* cups altogether. Also make sure you have extra cups for visitors.

+ Use environmentally-friendly dish soap in your office kitchen.
+ If possible recycle your toners.
+ Bring batteries to recycling depots in your office or town.
+ When ordering catering, order *real cutlery* and plates and avoid using disposables.
+ Make sure the lights are off when you leave, as well as your computers (check with your IT Department to see if turning your computer off is an option in your office).
+ Make sure you have a tray nearby for pages that have a lot of white space on them. You may be able to get it bound by a print shop and use them as note pads (banner pages from print jobs are excellent for this).
+ If you have magazine subscriptions that you no longer require, cancel the subscription.
+ If people have left the organization, make sure any mail you receive for them is returned to sender and let the company know to take this person off their distribution list.
+ If you have the opportunity to check your boss's mail, and you notice that he throws magazines out, or gets a lot of *generic letters* from companies, if agreeable, ask that he or she be taken off the mailing list.
+ In the winter open the blinds during the day and close them at night and do the opposite in the summer.
+ Take the stairs instead of the elevator when possible -- it's healthier for you too.
+ If you are in a position to suggest this, encourage people to teleconference or videoconference instead of travelling.

Chapter 13

I Gave at the Office: Charities in the Workplace

I remember as a child going door to door with my sister to collect for a charity. They had a volunteer instruction sheet we were supposed to read before canvassing. I still remember one thing that was written on it. "This charity does not collect from people at work." If anyone said "my husband gave at the office," we were to explain the error of that thinking.

Now fast forward to today. Workplace charities are becoming very popular and the charities are benefitting. We really are giving at the office.

Here are some ways I have seen charities supported in the workplace:

- Office Charity Campaigns
  - Some offices participate in raising money by having silent auctions, bake sales or any number of creative ways.
  - Contributing through payroll deductions.
  - Employers can participate as well by matching employee funds or by offering a day off to employees as an incentive for employee contributions.

- Sponsoring children in a third-world country through office donations.

- Global Tragedies

- o We are part of the global community and it is great to see offices playing a role in helping where there is a need when disaster strikes.
- ◆ Walk or run events to support specific causes
  - o We can be involved by sponsoring our co-workers or participating ourselves.
- ◆ Locally
  - o One office I worked for was involved in building a house for a needy family. It was a group effort with everyone doing something to help.
  - o Buying or selling chocolate bars or other products to support school programs.
  - o Supporting our local hospitals by volunteering or making a donation.
- ◆ Dress-down Fridays (50/50 Draw)
  - o Paying for the privilege to wear jeans on Friday with proceeds going to support local charities.

We should not be made to feel pressured to participate in workplace charities, it needs to be voluntary.

I believe when we are contributing to worthy causes together it makes the office feel a part of the community we live in.

Chapter 14

Sayings That Can Help You While You Work

I was listening to a little girl on the bus one morning singing, "A, B, C, D - L, M, N, O, P - W, X, Y, and Z." She didn't get all the letters right, but the alphabet song reminded me about all the little sayings that I have in my head that help me to remember rules we were taught in school about spelling, grammar and other subjects. Even though these rules do have exceptions, I still use them and they *do* help. Here are some that I use a lot. Maybe I've even made up a few of my own over the years.

Remember *i before e except after c*? I'm sure we have all seen that commercial about the man and woman debating this saying. We were shown the exceptions to this rule in that funny advertisement, "Rottweiler, weird, beige...." When I type a word with *ie* in it, I do find myself quoting this little saying to myself to check my spelling.

What about, *30 days has September, April, June and November, all the rest have 31 excepting February which has 28 days clear, 29 days each leap year*. If you don't have a calendar in front of you this one is a necessity.

Three letters and under use lower case, four letters and up use first letter caps. I was taught this as a rule for capitalization of headings when you are using initial caps. For example in the following heading it would be: Initial Caps in a Heading, but there are exceptions to this rule.

The first word in your heading should always have an initial cap no matter how many letters in the word.

Spell out numbers under 10 (one, two, three...) Ten and over use numerals (10, 11, 12...). I was taught this rule for writing out numbers and it *will* help you in your day-to-day writing, but again there are exceptions.

For filing alphabetically I was taught this general rule, *Nothing comes before Something.* For example: Smith, P. comes before Smith, Patrick, but as my teacher in high school used to say, "When in doubt, look in the phone book." The phone book is filed alphabetically and you can always use that as a reference. Now maybe that was a saying my high school teacher learned in her generation that she was passing on, but it also has exceptions.

I or me?

This is not really a saying, but something someone taught me that I always use when trying to figure out whether to use *I* or *me*.

I once worked in an office with a former grade-school grammar teacher (which is a good person to work with in our profession). She taught me an easy way to remember when to use *I* or *me* in a sentence. She said, "If you can change the sentence around and use *we* or *us* you can easily determine whether you need to use *I* or *me*." For example, in the sentence "We went to the store," the correct use would be "Brenda and I went to the store." In the sentence, "Do you want to go to the store with us?" the correct use would be, "Do you want to go to the store with Brenda and me?"

Therefore, if you can change the sentence around and use *we*, then the correct use would be *I* and if you can change the sentence around and use *us*, then the correct use would be *me*.

* *

TIME OUT

Hangers on

While walking from the bus to my office building one morning, I noticed a woman in front of me with a coat hanger hanging on the back of her coat. Obviously, she didn't realize it was there, but I was wondering to myself how she could have sat on the bus and not noticed. I thought somebody ought to tell her so I caught up to her to let her know and it turned out to be someone from my own office.

When I told her she had a hanger on her back, she thought I was joking. To humour me she reached back and with a look of surprise and dismay slowly brought out the metal coat hanger.

It was a great way to start the day, and when the people at the office found out we all had a good laugh.

* *

TIME OUT

Skeleton staff

I was part of the skeleton staff in my office between Christmas and the New Year. *Skeleton staffers* are a very interesting group of people. We wore jeans! Don't tell anyone as that is not allowed on any day other than Friday. We are obedient in this rule at every other time of the year, but at this in-between time we are emboldened because we are the *skeletons* and we know we can get away with it.

At one place I worked they even provided pizza and pop to reward us for this sacrifice we were making so everyone else could take the time off. We are a very humble group of volunteers. You should consider joining us some time. Of course if you do then we will probably stay home so you will be better able to appreciate this special role you can play in your office.

PART VII – SECRETARIAL TOOLBOX

Chapter 1

Blue, Black or Red Ink? Which Is better?

A good tip for signing a document is to sign it in blue ink. If you sign in black it is hard to tell which is the original and which is the photocopy.

I personally prefer my boss to use blue ink to make revisions to a document as well. I find I can see the changes better than with black ink. I had one boss who would make changes in pencil. I think I started needing glasses after working for that person. I would not recommend using pencil.

How can the assistant influence their boss to use a pen colour that is easier on the eyes? I only provide my boss with blue pens. Problem solved. When using red ink, see Part II, Chapter 11 on colour blindness.

Business Writing and Short Forms

*I*n writing, it all depends on your audience whether you use short forms. In personal e-mails and letters I will write contractions such as don't, can't, doesn't, etc., but in a business letter that is a no-no and I always spell the words out because business writing is more formal.

E-mail can be less formal. In an internal e-mail I will use short forms and acronyms, but when writing an e-mail to a client outside of my company I am more formal and write the words out.

I only use popular e-mail short forms like GB, OMG and LOL in personal e-mails.

If I am transcribing a dictation and my boss says the word *don't* in a sentence, I automatically change it to *do not* as I know he expects this of me. My job as the assistant is to make the letter or e-mail look professional and that includes correcting grammar, spelling and punctuation when necessary.

Chapter 3

Carbon Copies

ack in the 70's, when we typed a letter we would manually feed three pages in the typewriter. My electric typewriter was very high-tech at the time. The first page was letterhead, the second page yellow paper and the third page blue paper with a carbon paper in between each. The copies were commonly referred to as the *yellows* and *blues*.

When we typed on the original it would be copied onto the yellow and blue pages by the carbon paper. Hence the expression *carbon copy*. Today we still use the cc. It is sometimes referred to as a *courtesy copy*, but I still hear the term *carbon copy* as well.

The most common way to type it is: c.c., but I have also seen it c:, cc: or c. The same applies if you are referring to a blind carbon copy. It would be written as bcc:, b.c. or b.c.c.

Please note

The b.c.c. is not added to the original letter, but only the copy. You do not want the person to whom you are writing to know who you are copying. You would also have it on the file copy so you have a record of who you blind copied the letter to.

Chapter 4

Double-click to Show White Space

Recently I discovered a little something in Word that I had never noticed before. If you are in the View *Print Layout*, normally there is a space between each page. For example, at the bottom of a page the page will end and then there will be a small space and a new page will begin. Sometimes, however, there is a black line separating the two pages and my boss and I were wondering why.

If you put your cursor on the black line a little arrow icon will appear. Double-click on the arrow icon and the space will reappear, double-click again and it will change back to the black line. It will toggle back and forth by double clicking. So the next time you notice you have the black line and want to change it back to the space, you will know how to do it.

I have to wonder why they even give you the choice of one or the other, but this is how it works for those who want to know.

Chapter 5

E-mail Tip for Mass E-mailing

I copied many of my friends and acquaintances on an e-mail. One of those recipients then took the names from my list and started e-mailing my contacts for sales purposes. Lesson learned, but if that had been a business e-mail the consequences would have been more serious.

If you are sending a large mailing to contacts from different companies, consider putting their e-mail addresses in the b.c.c. section. That way nobody will see who else is getting the e-mail or have access to their e-mail address. This is particularly important in a business mass e-mail mailing.

Tips:

Some companies have firewalls to control the mass e-mails that come into their organization. By sending mass e-mail mailings their organization's firewall may start to recognize your e-mail address as spam and not allow any future e-mails to get through. To avoid this, some companies contract their mass mailings out to a marketing company.

I would not recommend requesting a Read Receipt on a large e-mailing or you will find your Inbox bombarded with Read Receipts.

Chapter 6

Face Up or Face Down?

I received some blank faxes and then got a phone call from an apologetic manager saying she was sorry about the faxes, but she rarely had to send a fax and when she did she was never quite sure whether to feed the paper face up or face down. I suggested a simple solution would be to get her staff to put a label on the fax machine to indicate *Feed face up* or *Feed face down*, whichever was appropriate. She was very appreciative and said she was going to get someone to do that for her.

I understood her frustration. At one place I worked you had to feed the paper face up on the photocopier, face down on one fax machine and face up on the other two fax machines.

The label solution was something I saw in our Mailroom. Simple, but if nobody thinks to do it, then blanks will be sent by those less familiar with the equipment.

Another good idea is to post instructions on how to send a fax and how to use the photocopier next to the machines. This is especially helpful for those who may need to use it after hours or on weekends.

Most fax machines and photocopiers do have small symbols to indicate whether the paper is to be fed face up or face down, but if you are not familiar with using the Mailroom equipment and are in a hurry this may not be as evident as a label.

Chapter 7

How to Remove the Date and Time Stamp From a PowerPoint Printout

*T*here is a date and time stamp on a PPT printout that you may not want. To remove it:

+ *File – Print*
+ *Preview* (at bottom left)
+ *Options* (top right)
+ Choose *Header Footer*
+ Under Tab *Notes & Handouts* or *Slide* (depending on what you want to print), unclick *Date and Time* and click *Apply to All.*

In Microsoft 2007 instead of File you press the Office Button which is located at the top left-hand corner of the screen.

Tip:

If you are printing your PPT presentation in black and white you should set the print function to black and white for the best print quality.

+ *File – Print*
+ *Color/grayscale* (at bottom left)
+ If you drop down the menu you will have a choice of colour, grayscale or pure black and white
+ Choose *black and white*

Chapter 8

Insert Symbols: Quick Keys for Accents

*H*ere are a few quick keys for some letters with accents and other useful symbols:

é = Ctrl ' (apostrophe) then press e

ç = Ctrl , (comma) then press c

¢ = Ctrl / (slash) then press c

If you want capital letters with accents, simply highlight the letter and choose *Change Case*. In Microsoft 2007 *Change Case* is located under the *Home* tab under *Font* [Aa].

You can also access these and many other symbols by choosing *Insert, Symbol* and then you have your choice of different symbols and letters.

Chapter 9

Is it Email or E-mail and Does it Matter?

*T*he full name is electronic mail and I have seen it written either email or e-mail. E-mail is the more correct way of writing it.

Whichever way you choose to write it you need to be consistent throughout your document. Your company may even have a preference on how they want it written.

Chapter 10

Is it One Space or Two?
Is it Ms. or is it Ms?

I t used to be that when you ended a sentence you put two spaces before starting the next sentence. Today I notice they use only one space between sentences. It also used to be that after a title you would put a period (i.e. Mrs. Ms. Mr. Dr.) but today I notice that the period is often dropped in favour of just Mr or Ms, but whichever way you write it, be consistent. Some companies specify in their office policies the way they want their documents to go out.

Chapter 11

Keeping Things Confidential

*M*ost of us work in a cubicle and it is easy for people to see what is on our computer screen or on our desk. Some things we work on are confidential and are not for everyone's eyes (including our co-workers). Here are some simple steps to keep things confidential:

- File documents, don't leave them lying around.
- Lock your filing cabinets.
- Turn paper over on your desk, clear your screen or lock your computer if someone comes by when you are working on something confidential.
- Don't talk to others about confidential information.

Always lock your computer when you leave your desk area!

Locking your computer

You can lock your computer by holding down the *Windows* key and the *L* key or by pressing *Ctrl Alt Delete* and then choose *Lock this computer*.

Chapter 12

Latin Anyone?

*H*ere are a few Latin words that will come in handy if you work in a legal office:

+ *bona fide* means *good faith.*
+ *prima facie* means *first glance.*
+ *res judicata* means *been determined.*
+ *res ipsa loquitor* means *the thing speaks for itself.*
+ *ex facie* means *on the face of it.*
+ and *et cetera* is Latin meaning *other things of that type.*

When Latin words are used in a document they should be *italicized.*

Chapter 13

Lonely Signature Lines

I was taught that you never leave the signature line on the last page on its own. You either carry some text over with it (at least two lines) or reformat the letter so the signature line fits with the other text.

I never suggest using less than 11 pt for your font size to make the letter fit all on one page. It is always preferable to use 12 pt.

Chapter 14

Male or Female?

I'm sure you have had to send a letter to someone and you just couldn't figure out by the name whether you are sending to a male or a female. So how do you address the letter?

I would suggest putting the person's first name and last name and then the address, and for the salutation I would suggest Dear and then the person's first name and last name.

Outlook Memory Tip

*O*utlook has a feature that remembers e-mail addresses you have used. When you begin to type an e-mail address it will bring up similar choices in a drop-down, assuming they might be the one you want to use. But sometimes these are e-mail addresses that have come back undeliverable as you had a typo in the address, or it's an old e-mail address for someone who has since moved to another company and you don't want these old addresses to pop up. To get rid of the incorrect address when it pops up, just move down with the arrow key to the address you want to delete and when it is highlighted press delete. It's as simple as that to get rid of it.

If you highlight and click the e-mail address or press *Enter* it will use that address. This also works the same in the cc and bcc sections of your e-mail message.

Chapter 16
Point Taken:
The Overuse of Exclamation Marks!!!

When I first started writing, if I wanted to make a point, I would use an exclamation mark! I guess I had a lot of points to make because when I look back at my earlier articles there are a lot of exclamation marks.

It was pointed out to me that this was a common mistake, but the more you use them the less effective they become. A period makes the point, without using an exclamation mark.

Chapter 17

Quick Tips Using Shortcut Keys

The shortcut keys can be great time savers. Here are a few that you might find useful:

When you are in a document and press Ctrl F2, it will bring you to *Print Preview*. Press Ctrl F2 again and it brings you back to your original view.

For line spacing highlight the text and then press Ctrl 1 for single space, Ctrl 2 for double space and Ctrl 5 for 1.5 spacing. I like to use this one.

I love using the shortcut keys. Your hands never have to leave the keyboard. Some of my favourites are:

- Ctrl a to select the entire document
- Ctrl u for underline
- Ctrl s to save
- Ctrl n to open a new document
- Ctrl i for italics
- Ctrl b for bold
- Ctrl p for print
- Ctrl f for find
- Ctrl c for copy
- Ctrl x for cut
- Ctrl v for paste...and there are many more

The more you use shortcut keys the easier it becomes to remember them. For a listing of these go on the Microsoft Help and Support website by pressing the F1 key and type in the words *shortcut keys*.

Here are some others I like:

+ Ctrl End to get to the end of a document.
+ Ctrl Home to get to the top of a document.
+ Ctrl Shift End will highlight everything from that point down to the end of the document.
+ Ctrl Shift Home will highlight everything from that point up to the top of the document.

Quick tip for changing case

Highlight a word or phrase and press Shift F3 and it will change the case, press Shift F3 again and it changes to another case. This works in Word and PowerPoint, but doesn't seem to work in Excel.

Quick tip for changing font size

Highlight a word or phrase and press Ctrl + Shift and use the *less than* key (<) or *greater than* key (>) to change your font size smaller or larger.

Quick tip for using superscript and subscript

Highlight a word or number and press Ctrl and the plus sign (+) for subscript. Press Ctrl + Shift and the plus sign (+) for superscript. You can toggle this key to change it back.

* * * * * * * * * * * * * * * * * * *

TIME OUT

When in doubt *right click*

I have found that when you are trying to find out how to do something in a document and can't seem to come up with the answer, try right clicking. When all else fails, it will usually be the answer.

Chapter 18

Return to Sender,
Who Do You Return It To?

Most business envelopes have a logo and business address pre-printed on the envelope, but if you are in a large organization with many people sending letters out every day, how will your Mailroom staff know who to give the envelope to if it comes back Return to Sender? A good tip is to put your boss's initials under the logo and address on the envelope. Depending on the size of your organization you may even need to put their full name.

If the envelope is returned, your Mailroom will know who sent it and can return it to the proper person. This is especially helpful when you are doing a large mail out because there is usually some mail returned.

Another reason to put the author's initials or name on the envelope is so the Mailroom staff will know who the author is and can return it for correction if they notice an error.

Chapter 19

Signing on Someone's Behalf

This is the normal practice I have seen for signing on someone's behalf:

Type their usual signature line, sign your name above it and handwrite *for* beside their typewritten name. It is also acceptable to use *per* or *p.p.*

Some things to consider:

- Have you been given authority to sign on their behalf?
- Does your company have a policy on the style they want used for signing for someone else?

Chapter 20
Tabbing Within a Table in Word

 T abbing within a table works great. Pressing the tab key will take you from one cell to the next, and if you are at the end of your table it will automatically create another row. But what if you want to tab within a cell? Ctrl Tab will let you tab within a cell, without going to the next cell.

Telephone Messages

I send telephone messages to my boss by e-mail rather than writing it on a telephone message pad. That way it won't get lost in the pile on their desk and saves on paper. You can also open a folder in Outlook called Telephone Messages to save the messages if that would be useful to refer back to.

The Little Yellow Sticky

What would we do without the little yellow sticky? Here are a few things I use them for:

- flagging pages in a book.
- reminder notes to myself which I stick on my computer.
- quick instructions or questions to my boss on correspondence or a file.
- if a co-worker is not at their desk and I need them for something, I leave a sticky on their computer screen or door with a quick note to call me.
- at home I put a reminder on my alarm clock or front door if I need to remember to do something that day.

The yellow sticky is meant for temporary use only. Don't depend on it if you need something more permanent.

Using AutoCorrect in Word

I am always looking for shortcuts and I found a neat way to speed up my typing using AutoCorrect.

For example, here are a few I have created.

If I type sbc and press the spacebar (or press enter) it automatically types SENT BY COURIER. Here are some others I use:

- sbf - SENT BY FACSIMILE
- sbr - SENT BY REGISTERED MAIL
- p&c - PERSONAL & CONFIDENTIAL

You can create an AutoCorrect for as many words as you like, but unless they are simple you will tend to forget your shortcut. I use mine often, and because they are the initials, they are very easy to remember. So try and keep it simple.

Creating an AutoCorrect shortcut in Word

- Go under *Tools – AutoCorrect - Replace:* sbc *With:* SENT BY COURIER

Create as many as you like, then press OK and you are set.

Microsoft 2007 instructions are as follows

In the Customize Quick Access Toolbar located at the top left-hand corner of your screen, click on the arrow down.

+ Choose *More Commands*
+ Choose *Proofing*
+ Click on *AutoCorrect Options*
+ Ensure *Replace Text as you Type* is clicked on
+ In the *Replace* box type in your short form, for example sbc
+ In the *With* box type in SENT BY COURIER
+ Press *Add*

Tip:

I use sbc instead of SC because SC is also a short form for South Carolina and if you don't pay attention you may have SENT BY COURIER in an address where you really wanted the state SC. So I add the *b* to avoid that.

Voting Buttons

A dding voting buttons to your e-mail message is useful if you are sending a message that requires people to respond to a question and you want to track the responses.

For example, if you are having an internal training session and have a choice of times to attend, you can send an e-mail with the details of the sessions along with some choices. The recipient just has to click on the appropriate voting button to respond. Once they make their choice they will be given the option to *send the message now* or *edit it before sending* and they can add an additional message if they like.

If you are organizing an office function and need to know how many will be attending, you might want to send an e-mail with voting buttons asking if they are planning to attend. The choices could be a simple Yes, No or Maybe for the answer.

It is a quick way to get responses and is very convenient for the sender who can then track the responses. I have set out below how to add voting buttons to your e-mail message and how to track them for those who are not familiar with this feature in Outlook 2007.

Add voting buttons to a message

+ In the message, click *Options*.
+ Select *Use Voting Buttons*. If the options they provide are not what you want choose *Customize*. When you press *Customize* make sure under *Voting and Tracking Options* the *Use Voting Buttons* is clicked

on. Type the voting button words you want to use in the box. Separate by a semi-colon with no space between each choice, i.e. Monday 3 p.m.;Monday 4 p.m.

+ Click *Close* and then write your message.
+ Choose your recipients and press *Send*.

Review tracking results and voting responses

+ Open the original message you are tracking. This message is usually located in the *Sent Items* folder.
+ Click the *Tracking* tab to see who has responded and what their response is. The *Tracking* tab will not be activated until someone responds and you have opened the message.

Note:

It has been my experience that voting buttons do not always work on external e-mails. You may want to do a test e-mail to a friend outside your organization to make sure this works before doing this type of e-mail to a client or outside contact.

* *

Constant reminders

You've heard of telephone tag, but have you heard of reminder tag? Maybe it is just me, but I seem to always be setting reminders. My boss asks me to get him some information, so I send a request to someone and set a reminder to follow up with them. They receive my request and while they are looking into it they set a reminder to get back to me. My boss then sets a reminder to follow up with me as to whether I have heard back from the other person and have the information for him. We are all setting reminders for the same thing.

I am going to have to set a reminder to talk to my boss about setting reminders.

PART VIII – OFFICE ETIQUETTE POEMS

By Lynn Crosbie

The Interview

You're going on an interview
Whether by choice or necessity
You have to go in with confidence
And being prepared is the key
When they say, "Tell me about yourself"
That's not the time to babble
Don't talk about your kids and spouse
Or your financial trouble

You could be asked things like
"What have you learned from your mistakes?"
Or "Why should we hire you
Over the other candidates?"
Where do you see yourself in five years
That's a good question
Or how do you handle a difficult co-worker
Or a stressful situation?

Try to stay calm and relaxed
Show them your great personality
They're also looking for a good fit
With the employees in their company
When they ask you a question
Take the time to think about it
They won't hold that against you
And you will benefit

You want a new job
But is this the right one for you
Find out about the organization
And be sure to ask questions too
What the work hours are
And what computer programs they use
But wait, don't quit your job just yet
Until an offer's been made to you

Filing

A lot of paper to file
Or maybe it's just one
Do something every day
And eventually you'll get it done
It may be hard to get motivated
And you want to leave it alone
But tomorrow's another day
And there's more paper to come

If your desire to continue
Gets slightly diminished
Continue to forge ahead
You'll feel better when it's finished
Filing is something
We all have in our workplace
Electronic or paper
Eventually there's a file we need to trace

There's a sense of achievement
You don't want to miss
When you can find a file
In five seconds or less
Whether it's numerical or alpha
Is your choice to make
But not having a good filing system
Is a big mistake

E-mail Etiquette

I received an e-mail from a colleague of mine
It was set in a background of yellow and lime
The font it was blue, almost impossible to see
And it was all in caps...was she yelling at me?

She had a few mistakes in that message as well
It got me to wondering if she could even spell
Covered with smiley's and little pictures too
Not too professional is the impression I drew

Most backgrounds are busy and take up lots of space
And not really appropriate for the workplace
Spell Check should be used, you should take the time
Organize your e-mail regularly so you don't get behind

Save the smiley's, jokes and pictures for use at home
And if you have bad news best to use the phone
Simple rules to follow, common sense things to do
Remember your organization is being represented by you

Meetings

So you've organized a meeting
Arranged the venue, time and date
You've sent the details
And hope nobody is late
You've checked to make sure
The *key* people can attend
While other members arrange
For a delegate to send

You've ordered the catering
And hope people like the food
You've checked out the A.V.
And everything is good
You've copied all the handouts
You've placed them on the chairs
Everyone has good directions
No problems getting there

You've made travel arrangements
For your out-of-town guests
And you've booked a hotel
So they have a place to rest
You've sent them their Itinerary
And the confirmations too
You've kept within budget
And paid the bills before they're due

You've made all your deadlines
With the help of to-do lists
You wanted to make sure
That nothing got missed
Working behind the scenes
Taking great care
To make sure everything is perfect
And everyone is there

Gossiping in the Workplace

If your workplace buddies
Are *gossip friends*
Are they really someone
You can trust in the end?
You think they're your friend
And won't talk about you
But do you honestly believe
That to be true?

People who gossip
Like to dig for *dirt*
They may go too far
And someone gets hurt
They bring up rumours
And hearsay too
But do you really care
Even if it were true?

Forget the meaningless chitchat
And foolish chatter
Stop the gossiping
And talk about things that matter
Do unto others
I'm sure you've all heard
And if you can't say something nice
Don't say a word

Gossiping in the workplace
Is something to avoid
Don't do it to fit in
Or if you are bored
The way to stop gossiping
Is to not participate
Just go about your business
And don't help spread hate

Patricia Robb

The Office Fridge

The office fridge can be a mess
Something has spilt, something's been left
That plastic container has been there a year
No one will open it, out of fear

Expiry dates have long been ignored
Drinks are lined up on the door
Is it yours or is it mine?
I can't remember if I brought that kind

Lots of lunches there to see
That one's green though -- should it be?
The office fridge can be a friendly place
If people don't abuse the space

If you put in a lunch, be sure to claim
And identify with date and name
Clean out the fridge when you have time
And make Fridays the *throw-out* deadline

PART IX (A) - THE REST OF YOUR LIFE: KEEPING A BALANCE

"Twenty years from now you will be more disappointed by the things that you didn't do than by the ones you did do. So throw off the bowlines. Sail away from the safe harbour. Catch the trade winds in your sails. Explore. Dream. Discover."

MARK TWAIN

Chapter 7

Before and After Work

There is more to life than work, but work is a big part of it and we spend a good portion of our time there. How can we make the rest of our life a bit simpler and how can we make sure we are taking care of ourselves as we take care of business?

Parents tend to come home from work only to start work again with taking care of their children, helping them with homework, driving them to various clubs and activities, volunteering at schools or charities, making meals, preparing lunches, and on the weekend there is always the house-cleaning, grocery shopping and the laundry to do. If you are a single parent this can be even busier because you are doing it all yourself. Empty nesting and retirement never sounded so good.

If you are single, life can also be busy after work with taking courses, doing volunteer work, social activities and family responsibilities, to name a few.

Add to all this that we are the 24/7 generation of working late and working at home and on the road. We need to take the time to relax and take care of ourselves physically, emotionally and spiritually.

The next few chapters are not about work – Enjoy!

Chapter 2

Taking Care of Ourselves: Making Time for Exercise

An ACE commissioned study found that secretaries, teachers, lawyers and police officers walked significantly fewer steps and less distance than other occupations. At the low end, secretaries were observed to walk only an average of 4,327 steps. The recommended goal being 10,000 steps a day.

I am a firm believer in finding time in your day for at least 30 minutes of exercise. It will improve your health and perhaps even your productivity. Finding time for fitness is not always an easy task, but I have found going to the gym on my lunch hour has been the best time. Others in my office go first thing in the morning or after work. When you go or what you do is not important, the important thing is to get some kind of exercise every day. I have written about my experiences at the gym and I hope it will encourage you to keep on keeping on.

Quitting is not an option

I had been going to the gym for three years with no results. I was discouraged. I wasn't gaining weight, but I wasn't losing any either. Where were all the toned muscles I had expected? I was also getting bored with

---

* American Council on Exercise ("ACE"), Press Release, http://www.acefitness. org/media/media_display.aspx?NewsID=265 (accessed February 18, 2008)

the same routine. So I did what many people do after their initial zeal – I quit!

I browsed around looking for another fitness place where I might be more motivated. At one gym I saw a sign-up sheet for a personal trainer. Could I afford it? It was expensive, but they promised results. I was turning 50 that year. It seemed every decade brought on five more pounds of unwanted fat. This time I was ready to do battle. I signed up.

I went into it with high expectations and determination. I, of course, wanted instant results, but was told it was going to take time and that I had to be committed and do the work.

I signed up for 12 weeks. I was faithful. I worked hard and was going to the gym three times a week. I started to see some results and lost five pounds. I listened to the trainer as he told me about my diet and what I should and shouldn't eat. My muscles were getting toned, I could see the difference. But I was hoping to lose more weight than that.

Now the 12 weeks were up and I was on my own, but this time I was equipped with the knowledge the trainer had given me so I continued to work out. I added 20 minutes of cardio on my weight training days and on the alternate days I did a 30-minute cardio work out. I could still hear my trainer saying, "Just five more, come on I know you can do it." I committed to going to the gym a minimum of five times a week with the weekend being my break time.

I have now lost 15 pounds. I went from a size 12 to a size 8. I have my shape back. My muscles are more defined. I am more comfortable in this body of mine and I feel fit. Some of my co-workers tell me I've inspired them to work out. They can see the difference.

I would recommend going to a personal trainer, at least for a short time. You will get educated on what you need to do to accomplish your goals. The weight machines won't seem so frightening. They will become familiar and easy to use. Most of all you will have a plan.

I had almost bored myself out of going to the gym from those first three years when I didn't know what I was doing. I had one routine that I did every time I went. It is no wonder people drop out and decide it is not for them.

My routine is now varied. I change things up and try to make my time at the gym interesting. I challenge myself. No, I didn't lose the weight I thought I would with the trainer, but I did gain something much more valuable – I got educated on how to use the gym.

So join a gym, go for a walk, climb the stairs each day, do something and keep healthy.

Check it out...

Most gyms offer corporate discounts. Check with the gym when you sign up or with your HR Manager as your office may have a partnership with a gym. Our firm did not have a corporate discount so I applied for one. It was an easy process and resulted in a savings for my co-workers.

Tip:

In order to make the time pass quickly on the treadmill or elliptical machine, I use my songs on my MP3 player to gauge my time. For example if I want to run for 30 minutes, that is approximately five or six songs. I pick my favourite music then concentrate more on the music than I do on the running and in no time I have run the 30 minutes.

* *

TIME OUT

Office confidential

I went to the gym after work on a Friday evening. I had a great workout and went back to the office to get my purse and things to bring home. I always take my gym laundry home on Friday to wash over the weekend. On Monday morning as I was madly trying to get out the door, I couldn't find my gym clothes. Did I not bring them home? Where were they? I left for work thinking perhaps I had left them in my gym bag at work. When I walked into the office and got to my desk, there they were, on my desk with my bra sitting right on top of the bundle.

Chapter 3

Hair Care

I am a licensed hairdresser as well as an administrative assistant. I worked as a hairdresser for five years before returning to the office. I never regretted the training I had in hairdressing as it has been a useful skill to have. I continue to cut and colour hair for family and friends. I have written a few helpful hints for hair care that I hope you will find useful.

Colour removes colour

As a hairdresser we were taught early on that colour removes colour. On a chat line I was on someone wrote that they had coloured their hair and had gotten some on their arm and now they had a brown stain and wondered how they could remove it. If she had taken some of the excess colour and rubbed it on the stain it would have removed it. The same applies for the colour that gets on your face around the hairline. Take some of the remaining colour, or use your hair with the colour already on it, and rub your hairline and it will remove the stain. Then quickly use a tissue or a cloth to remove the excess colour so it won't start to stain again.

Too many chemical treatments

If you perm your hair you shouldn't colour it as well. You can do one or the other, but I would not recommend doing both. If you insist on doing both, then using a professional shampoo and conditioner becomes a necessity.

Professional products

I always recommend using a professional shampoo and conditioner. I have heard people say many times that they love the feel of their hair after leaving the salon. Having your hair washed with a good quality shampoo and conditioner makes a big difference.

The professional product is not as expensive as you might think, and the quality of the product is much better. The professional product is also concentrated so you don't have to use as much. Your hairdresser will be able to recommend the right product for your hair type.

Off-the-counter dandruff shampoos are very hard on your hair. There are professional products that will help control dandruff and won't be as harsh. Talk to your hairdresser. If you have psoriasis or seborrhoea you will need to discuss treatment options with your doctor.

We were taught in hairdressing school that dandruff is caused by a parasite. It has been my experience that what many people think is dandruff, is not dandruff at all. When I have had flaking skin on my scalp it is more likely caused by a hair product or it is a result of dry skin. When I changed the product to something with little or no perfume the flaking disappeared.

Using a good professional shampoo on your baby will lessen and can even eliminate cradle cap. There are some good products made just for babies. If you have extra sensitive skin you might try using these products on yourself as well.

More suds are not always better

We are used to suds and we tend to think our hair is not clean unless we see lots of it. When using a professional product it will not be as sudsy because there is no detergent in it, which is better for the hair.

To use shampoo correctly you should apply shampoo the size of a quarter on the palm of your hand (this will vary depending on the length of your hair). Rub your hands together and then spread the shampoo through your hair and wash as normal. People tend to plop the product on the top of their head and then rub it into their scalps.

I usually wash and rinse my hair twice before applying the conditioner. Use the same process to apply the conditioner. If you have chemically treated hair (perms and colours) I would double the portion of conditioner used.

Professional styling products

Any liquid professional styling product (or a mousse or gel) should also be put on the palm of your hand in a small quantity. Rub hands together and then run your fingers through your hair. Be sure to apply the product to your hair. These products are to help you style your hair, not to put on your scalp.

Good styling products will assist you to style your hair and get the look you want. Your hairdresser will be able to help you choose the proper styling products.

Hair stuff...

Hair on average grows half an inch a month. Women's hair tends to grow faster than men's hair and children's hair grows faster than an adult's hair.

Hair grows faster in the summer than in the winter. If you take a two-week trip down south and then notice your hair seems longer, it is not an illusion, it actually does grow faster in the warmer climate. Unfortunately that is also true for hair on your legs and elsewhere so you will have to shave more often or have those areas waxed before going on your trip. Electrolysis and laser treatments are also available, but are more expensive.

You can use hair conditioner on your legs to prepare for shaving. It will leave your legs silky smooth.

When making a ponytail in your hair, never use a rubber band as it will cause breakage. Use a covered elastic or a clip to tie your hair back.

* *

TIME OUT

Next customer please...

While I was cutting hair one day I noticed one of the other hairdressers going to the counter to greet a customer. I was expecting my next customer so I knew it could be him. After taking his name and asking him to have a seat, my co-worker called out to me, "Pat, your John is here."

PART IX (B) – HELP FROM A CHEF WITH HINTS, TIPS AND RECIPES FOR TODAY'S BUSY WORKER

My daughter was brought up in a working single parent household. As she entered her early teens she would prepare meals for us so we could sit down and have supper at a decent hour. It is no wonder that she wanted to be a chef. She jokes that she had to learn to cook because I couldn't, but she has always loved creating in the kitchen.

Here are some hints and tips and recipes from her to help us in our busy lives.

By Krysta Anstey

Chapter 4

Menu Planning 101: The Importance of Planning Ahead

You plan your day, why not plan your meals? Planning out a weeks worth of meals can save you time, effort and hungry bellies, as well as cut down on take out and waste from foods that don't get used.

The kitchen to-do list

I am not going to lie. I love lists. I make a list for just about anything that needs to be done. One of the first things I do before I start my workday in the restaurant is make a list of what products I will need and what prep I need to do. Once each item is completed, I cross it off my list.

I do the same thing at home. The best part about it is that no matter how busy our schedules, my husband and I get to sit down and have a meal together because we prepared ahead. It is very easy to do and will make mealtime more enjoyable.

Make a date with your cookbook

Grab a few food magazines, cookbooks or look at some websites. Bookmark your favourites then narrow it down. Look at similarities between the recipe ingredients. When you have chosen a few recipes you can use them to start your grocery list.

Maybe there is a recipe with an interesting spice you would like to try. Spices may be a little pricey, but they last for more than just one use so you will have them on hand in case you want to try that recipe again (or even get creative and use it in something else).

There are no rules to your recipes. Make them up as you go along. What if there is something in it you don't like? Substitute something else that you do like. Recipes are only a guideline for your taste buds.

Once you have written out your recipes in grocery list form, add all your regular items and off you go. The biggest part about planning your menu is done. Now all you have to do is buy the groceries and make the meals.

Getting started

Enjoy your time in the kitchen and use it as a time to be creative and have fun. If it is all work and no play it will just seem like another job you have to do. Involve your family in the preparation and make a day of it. The rewards for the week will be worth it and you will have spent some quality time with your family.

Once you are ready to start, make a list of what you will need and how long it will take to prepare it. You will find that your recipes will lend themselves to being prepped at the same time if you have taken the time to plan it out ahead of time.

The first thing to do is take out anything that needs to thaw, soak or slow cook. These things are going to take the longest so do them first. For example, soak the beans, thaw the ground beef, brown the stewing beef and set the slow cooker.

Once your prep is done and things are cooking, all your meals will be ready to portion out for the week. Your after-work time will then be just heating up your prepared meals and throwing a salad together or a vegetable dish which will make your weeknights much less stressful.

Chapter 5

Breakfast on the Go

Skipping breakfast to rush off to work? Too many times I have rushed out of the house, rushed back in to retrieve forgotten items and then rushed back out again. I run for the streetcar, manage to squeeze my way to the back, nab a seat and open a book only to be interrupted by my angry growling stomach. I forgot to eat breakfast again! Off to the coffee shop I go and order the usual, coffee and a croissant combo. One day, I promise myself, I will make time for a healthy breakfast, but here I am eating another bite of buttery goodness again.

As I was contemplating this routine of unhealthy eating, the thought struck me that "I have a blender" and the idea for healthier breakfasts began.

Breakfast Smoothie

1 cup plain low-fat yoghurt
1 cup orange juice
½ cup frozen unsweetened berries or fruit (blueberries, mixed berries or even mango)
2 tbsp. pure honey
1 banana

Mix until blended, pour and enjoy. You can add some protein powder for a good healthy breakfast.

Boiled Eggs & Smoked Salmon

Breakfast on the go doesn't have to be a hassle. If you pack a lunch, packing a breakfast isn't that hard. Boil an egg the night before. Maybe add some leftovers if you've got them. This is a great way to start your day and can all be eaten cold.

For an egg that is not too hard and not too soft, follow these steps:

Bring 1 pot of water to a boil
Add 1 tsp. of sea salt

When adding your eggs to the boiling water, be very careful. Take a pin and put a small hole in the bottom (the large side) of the egg. This will allow air to escape without the egg cracking. Hold the egg over the steam to gradually warm it up, then slowly immerse in the water.

Reduce heat to medium high and set timer for 6 minutes. Remove eggs and run under cold water. Put in a container with a few slices of smoked salmon. Some leftovers that you might consider adding to this breakfast are potatoes, beets, sour cream and chives, just little things to make it interesting.

Chapter 6

Choosing the Right Vinegar Can Be Compared to Choosing a Good Wine

Vinegar: derived from the French 'vin aigre' which means 'sour wine'

With so many choices it's little wonder people can get overwhelmed when choosing vinegars and oils. Many people usually end up skipping the choices and go right for the pre-made salad dressings. With just a few tidbits of information I hope to help clarify the confusion.

When choosing a vinegar think about how you would select a good wine. Age, flavour and region are all very important factors to consider. The range in quality is immense and there are so many to choose from.

Some of the best vinegars are made in the same regions as many of the best wines, such as balsamic from Modena Italy or sherry wine vinegar from Spain. These can be found in most specialty shops. The best part about going to a specialty shop is they usually allow a taste test, but whether they do or not, they certainly will be armed with knowledge about the product.

A good tip in choosing vinegar is the aroma. The aroma should suggest the wine or liquid it was derived from.

Aceto Balsamico is one of the more popular flavours of vinegar. Translated it is simply balsamic vinegar. It is named for its pleasant aroma. It is a mellow reddish brown vinegar that I find to be very versatile in many dishes. It is made by aging sweet wine for a long time in small wooden barrels. Balsamico is a wonderful vinegar to use in marinades, salad dressings, or just simply for dipping bread.

Champagne vinegar has a sweet light flavour with a hint of tartness. It is fermented from champagne and tastes lovely with things like honey, walnut oil and citrus.

Red wine vinegar can be made from any red wine. It has a sharp full-bodied sweet flavour. It pairs well with olive oil and is a great compliment to tangy greens such as arugula or rocket.

White wine vinegar like red wine vinegar can be fermented from any white wine, such as Chardonnay or Riesling. Mild greens like butter lettuce or red leaf lettuce are nice with this vinegar.

A few things I like to pair vinegar and oil with are:

- Roma tomatoes, basil, buffalo mozzarella drizzled with balsamico and olive oil, sea salt and cracked black pepper.
- Segments of orange and pink grapefruit, with tarragon on a bed of butter lettuce drizzled with champagne or white wine vinegar and walnut oil, sea salt and cracked black pepper.

I hope this will help you in making your choice of a good vinegar.

Chapter 7

Restaurant Etiquette

*H*ere are some etiquette tips when going to a fine-dining restaurant to make the experience more enjoyable for both you and the restaurant staff:

+ Don't snap your fingers for service. To get the attention of your server, you can motion them over with a wave of your hand, or ask a bus-person or another server if they would let your server know you are looking for them.

+ Don't be afraid to ask your server if you don't understand something on the menu.

+ Learn your server's name. Most servers will introduce themselves when they arrive at your table. Greet them with a warm hello and you will notice a more pleasant server eagerly wanting to serve your table. It is a win-win situation.

+ If you have a severe food allergy be sure to tell the kitchen staff and they will do their best to ensure your safety. On another note, if there is one ingredient you just don't like, please tell your server and they will remove it if possible.

+ If you were not happy with your service but really enjoyed your meal, please keep in mind when passing on a tip that in most places the kitchen will get a small percentage of that tip...if you want to send a message to the kitchen that you loved your meal, drinks will always be appreciated by an overheated kitchen staff at the end of a shift.

- Easy on the perfume. To really enjoy your meal you need to use all your senses. You don't want perfume interrupting your enjoyment of the meal or those sitting nearby.
- If the sign says please wait to be seated...please wait. There are maps and plans on how our chaos is organized, and only the maître d' knows how to orchestrate it. On the other hand, if the sign says please seat yourself, be sure to catch the attention of someone to make sure you aren't waiting too long. If there are clean tables please don't sit at the only dirty one. You would be surprised how many people do this.
- When you are ready to order place your closed menu at the side of the table. This is a sign for "I'm ready." When you are finished eating, place your cutlery on your plate. This will let your server know you are finished without them having to ask. The next time you are wondering what's taking so long, check your table to see what you could do to send a silent message.
- Writing your own menu: Don't do it! Some people will order something at a restaurant but by the time they have finished their order it has changed into their own creation, not ours. We work very hard at writing menus and doing prep and portioning our food. When you mix and match it throws things off. This will only stop the flow of production and make things slower.

Chapter 8

Sticky and Delicious BBQ Ribs

*T*his is most likely one of the easiest and tastiest recipes for BBQ ribs I have tried yet. Very simple and with so many variations, but this is the one that works best for me:

- 2 sides of pork back ribs (I cut each side in two. It makes it easier to marinade). Be sure to rinse the ribs, especially if they were in an airtight bag.

- Prepare Marinade:

- 2 tbsp. liquid smoke*, 1/2 cup grainy dijon mustard, 1/2 cup honey, 1/2 cup white vinegar, 1 cup water, 1 white onion quartered.**
    o *Liquid smoke can be purchased at the grocery store or any spe-cialty store. It is reasonably priced.
    o **PRESIDENT'S CHOICE® honey Dijon marinade sauce is an excellent product available at Loblaws. If using the President's Choice marinade sauce, use 1 full cup mixed with the liquid smoke. The results are the same, but it is an easier option.

- Submerse ribs fully in the liquid. Let marinate for at least 2 hours (of course overnight is ideal).

- Preheat oven to 350°F. Cook ribs in marinade for one hour. Remove from oven and discard excess marinade.

- Heat grill on med-high, place ribs meat side down for 2 minutes. Flip and coat with BBQ sauce (I like honey garlic flavour for these).

- Cook until the sauce is sticky.

Serve with corn on the cob and mashed potatoes for a real southern taste.

I can vouch that these ribs are delicious. I was served them not long ago and they were mouth-watering. Patricia

Sample Resume

Here is a sample resume that I use. Feel free to use it.

RESUME:

Co-ordinates (Name, Address , etc.)

OBJECTIVE:

[What is your objective? What kind of position are you looking for and what do you have to offer? Customize this paragraph to the job you are applying for. I was applying for a job in the legal environment so I wanted to highlight that experience.]

Administrative support utilizing strengths in typing, speed, accuracy, software programs and organization to provide high quality services to professional staff in a legal environment.

SUMMARY:

[Summarize your work experience]

- Almost 30 years of progressive achievement as a secretary in the legal, medical and high-tech fields
- Recent experience as a legal assistant in a major law firm
- Previous experience as a legal assistant to a corporate lawyer
- Highly skilled typist with excellent knowledge of various computer software programs

SKILLS AND STRENGTHS:

[List your computer skills (i.e. Word, Excel, etc.), but also your strengths. Some examples are listed below:]

+ Fast accurate typist
+ Ability to work with minimal supervision
+ Interpersonal skills and a team player
+ Organization skills
+ Hard worker
+ Reliable

ACCOMPLISHMENTS:

[Highlight some of your accomplishments and list any pertinent courses you have taken and don't forget to include this one...]

+ Maintained excellent attendance record

RECENT WORK EXPERIENCE:

Name of Employer and Job Title September 2004 - Present
Name of Employer and Job Title November 1996 – September 2004

PREVIOUS WORK EXPERIENCE:

[If you feel you need to include some of your older work experience (anything over 10 years) write a paragraph summarizing what you have done. If they want to know more, they can ask you at the interview.]

Secretarial experience in offices including [names of different companies you worked for].

EDUCATION:

[If your education is 20 years ago and only includes high school, I would recommend putting it after your Work Experience or not at all. Your work experience becomes more relevant if your education is too far in the past.]

LANGUAGE:

[Languages spoken]

REFERENCES AVAILABLE ON REQUEST

30 Interview Questions and Answers

I suggest you go over the following questions and practice answering them and get comfortable with the whole interview process. I am not always asked these particular questions, but it puts me in the *interview mode* by practising them. These answers are here to be used as a guide and a help. Use your own skills and experiences to come up with your answers.

1. **Tell me about yourself?**

   In this question they are asking you to briefly describe your background and experience. Be prepared with a five liner which describes you. Practice it with enthusiasm. The first few minutes of the interview, including your very first exchange with the staffing specialist, often forms a lasting impression and may mean getting the job or not. If you have an opportunity, do this on videotape and watch your body language. Do you appear confident? Are there too many *ahs* and *ums* in your speech pattern?

2. **What are your greatest strengths and what are your weaknesses?**

   You must be prepared to talk about your strengths and weaknesses. For weaknesses, do not say, "I don't like filing or answering the phone" if you are applying for an admin assistant job. You could say something like, "I am a perfectionist." This could be considered a weakness to you because you are hard on yourself and have high expectations, but I would consider this an asset to any company you would work for. Be aware of the overuse of this answer for weaknesses.

Another answer might be that you have a hard time accepting compliments for a job well done. This is a weakness for you, but would not affect your performance in any way.

Strengths on the other hand are easy. Your strengths are your skills. If you have advanced computer skills, be prepared to list them. If you say you have great organizational skills you need to be prepared to give examples of something you have organized. Capitalize on your greatest strengths.

3. **Do you work well under pressure? How do you handle it?**

I handle working under pressure by being organized. I prioritize what I need to accomplish and as I complete it I cross it off my list. I maintain a to-do list for all projects. If you are already an assistant I am sure you have had to handle stressful situations. How have you handled them? Do you remain calm? Are you organized? Think about those things and come up with your own answer to this question and your own examples.

4. **Are you a team player?**

I work in a department in which the assistants work together as a team. We know what needs to be done and we help each other to accomplish that. We have a common goal and we work together to meet the challenge. How about you? Do you work in a team? Do you work well with others? You can explain how you have worked as a team member with your supervisor, co-workers, other departments, other organizations, etc. Working in a team involves giving feedback, sharing ideas, collaborating with team members, sharing experiences and knowledge, being an effective listener, participating in meetings and discussions and being supportive and understanding. You have to answer these questions for yourself based on your own experiences.

5. **What do you see yourself doing five years from now?**

What are your goals? In my position I am seeking to acquire greater knowledge and skills so I can better assist the professional I work for. You have to personalize where you see yourself. You can also say that you hope you are effective in maintaining the high standards of the office and that you hope to gain the trust and respect of your supervisor and the department.

6. **Explain how you have shown initiative in a previous job.**

    Think about how you show initiative in your job. Do you go the extra mile or do you just do the task that you are given? I show initiative in my job by looking for ways to make my professional's job easier. I draft letters, get files, mark dates in the calendar. When I see something that needs to be done, I take the initiative to do it.

7. **What are five words that you would use to describe yourself?**

    Some examples are: team player, organized, sense of humour, punctual, quick learner. Find words that describe you.

8. **What makes you qualified for this job?**

    You can tell them about your years of experience, your skills and work you have done with minimal supervision. Tell them about your successes in previous jobs. Also, this is a good opportunity to talk about things that are not on your resume.

9. **What do you want me to know about you that is not on your resume?**

    Some examples could be:

    *   Helpful to others
    *   Initiative
    *   Resourceful
    *   Take pride in your work. Always taking the extra step to make sure the job is done to the best of your ability and seeing a project through to completion and on deadline
    *   Sense of humour
    *   Detail oriented
    *   Quick learner

10. **If you felt overwhelmed with the volume of your workload, what coping strategies would you use?**

    Some examples are:

+ Working through breaks or lunch
+ Coming in early
+ Staying late
+ Communicating with others on the team and your manager to make them aware of the situation
+ Getting help from other staff
+ Making sure you stay organized
+ Prioritizing (if necessary, ask your manager to prioritize what needs to be done first)

11. What will your references say about you?

Your references are people that you have chosen, therefore you should be able to say that they will have positive things to say about you. However, you may want to review with your referee what they will say about you. Ensure your references know they may get a call, from what company and the job applied for. A *ready* referee is the best kind. Don't forget to follow up with your referees, especially if you get the job. A thank you card is lovely to receive. They won't mind doing it again next time.

Some examples of what your referee might say:

+ Hard worker
+ Gets along with others
+ Team player
+ Experienced and knowledgeable about software
+ Shares knowledge and information
+ Initiative
+ Dependable

12. How do you like to be managed?

Personally, I like a manager who asks for my opinion and gives me feedback. I also like a manager who knows what they want to do with their department and have vision, as well as someone who is supportive and appreciative of the work I do. Ask this of yourself. What management style do you like best?

13. What do you dislike doing?

Don't say anything that will be seen as negative. You can say that you are prepared to do whatever it takes to get the job done well and on time.

14. You may be overqualified for this position?

Thank them for the compliment but say that if they feel you are overqualified, this will help you make a contribution to the organization sooner than someone with less experience. Emphasize that you are interested in <u>this</u> position.

15. What are you looking for in a job?

You could be looking for a job that is busy and challenging, or a long term opportunity in a growing organization where you can learn new skills and develop your present skills.

16. How much supervision do you need to complete a job?

You aren't expected to know everything right away, but they want to know that you have initiative and that you are a quick learner. Even after you've been on the job for awhile, occasional checks and getting feedback is always a good idea to ensure you are on the right track. You can tell them about any opportunities you have had to work with minimal supervision in previous jobs.

17. What personal qualifications and skills have helped you the most?

Use your own work experiences. Some that I have used are: I get along with others, I am flexible, I am a good listener, I am helpful, I am not afraid to ask questions and I am organized.

18. Describe a situation where you had to deal with a difficult person. What did you do?

Describing a difficult co-worker in past jobs is not necessarily what you should be talking about here. Your answer could be as simple as describing how you handled a call from someone who was very upset and difficult to deal with.

19. **If there are employment gaps in your resume, be prepared to explain them.**

    I have found that honesty is the best policy, but you do not need to go into detail unless you are asked for further information. We all have lives outside of work and sometimes we need to take some time off to either raise a family, care for an elderly or sick family member or any number of reasons. Be prepared to give a brief reason for your absence. Sometimes your reason can give the potential employer a glimpse into what type of person you are. As a single mom I took time off to raise my daughter, which was difficult financially, but I felt necessary. The person who interviewed me thought that what I had done was honourable and I ended up getting the job. I had the necessary skills for the job, but by being honest he was able to see that I was not only qualified, but was also a responsible and honest person, which are good qualities to have in an employee.

20. **Why should I hire you over the other candidates?**

    You could tell them about your years of experience, your skills, any opportunity you have had to work with minimal supervision on projects and your successes in previous jobs. Be prepared to back up anything you say with examples.

21. **How do you handle criticism?**

    I listen to the criticism and ask questions to make sure I understand and, if necessary, make changes. You can turn this question around and ask if they have regular performance appraisals in their organization since you feel it is important to get feedback on how you are performing in your job so you can improve in any areas that you need to.

22. **What do you think of the last company you worked for?**

    Don't say anything negative even if you are leaving on bad terms. There must be something you liked about the job. Examples could be that they had good training, good educational programs or that you liked your co-workers. Stress the positive aspects of your last company.

23. Why are you leaving the organization you work for now?

Explain the reason you are leaving, but don't mention anything negative. Maybe you are looking for a better paying job, or you have recently moved and want to be closer to your end of town, or you just want a change because your former job wasn't challenging enough.

24. How long do you think it would be before you were making a significant contribution to the company?

There is a learning curve with any new job and they don't expect you to come in and know what to do immediately, but they do want to hear that it won't be long before you are able to work on your own. You can explain that you are a quick learner and that you are looking forward to gaining the experience and knowledge necessary so that you can quickly become a reliable asset to their company. You can also ask them how soon they would expect it.

25. Give an example of something you organized and explain how you went about it?

Give an example of a successful project or event that you organized. I organize by using to-do lists which I keep updated with all of my deadlines, priorities, what needs to be done and who is doing what. Think about something you have organized and how you accomplished it.

26. How would you ensure your boss is organized?

Some examples might be having regular meetings with your boss to go over their calendar, having a good bring-forward system, organizing your boss's desk in a way that is suitable to both of you or setting up an efficient filing system. Keeping yourself organized will help your boss to be organized.

27. When working on multiple projects, how do you deal with conflicting priorities and demands?

Examples could be that you prioritize your activities and keep organized with the help of to-do lists for all projects as well as your regular workload. The to-do list helps you to keep track of all deadlines and priorities. You can also explain that when necessary you have no problem delegating to one of your other team members and you keep an open communication with your supervisor to discuss multiple deadlines and get their assistance with re-prioritizing if necessary, to ensure you keep to your schedule.

28. How would you rate your communication skills?

Explain how you effectively communicate in writing, on the phone and in person.

29. What makes you unique?

They are looking for something that sets you apart from the other candidates they have interviewed. Think of something that they will remember about you after the interview is over, i.e. your advanced computer skills, excellent attendance record and your personality and enthusiasm.

30. What motivates you?

We can be motivated by our working environment, our co-workers, a busy office and a job with good educational opportunities.

Questions YOU can ask in an interview

So many people recommend asking questions at an interview. What are some of the questions you can ask? A good interview is one that turns into a conversation, with them asking questions of you, but with you also asking questions of them. It will be more relaxing for both parties and by your questions you will give them a good idea about your expectations and capabilities and how you will fit in.

You can either write some questions down as the interview proceeds and ask them at the end of the interview or you can ask them after you have answered their question.

If you don't understand a question that is asked of you, don't be afraid to ask them to clarify it.

You need to play it by ear in the interview. Some questions that they ask you can be turned around into a question for them or can bring up a question in your mind about the position.

Things you can do before the interview

Do some research on the company where you are applying. Do you have any questions about the company or the department? By asking questions you show them you are interested in what they are doing as a company.

If you are called for an interview you should ask for a copy of the job description.

You should also look carefully at the job posting. Is there anything in the listing of duties that creates questions in your mind about the job? If there is anything you are not sure about and you have the opportunity to ask before the interview, that would be ideal, but it is also OK to bring these things up in the interview.

If they list a duty that you would like to know what the expectations would be, i.e. "some bookkeeping required" you should ask in the interview.

If they ask you if you are a team player, after you give your answer you might want to ask them what kind of a team environment their company promotes.

If they ask you what you would see yourself doing in five years, that would be a good opportunity for you to ask about the company's career development opportunities.

I would not bring up salary unless you are asked, but if they ask what salary you are looking for, you might turn the question around and ask them what they are offering. You can ask about their pay scale for the position and if there is room to grow.

Give Examples

If they ask you a question and you can give an example that would add to your answer, talk about it. For example, if they ask you if you are experienced at organizing conferences, you may want to tell them about some of the successful conferences you have organized.

Pay attention to the questions asked and if they create a question in your mind, or it brings up something you have done, don't be afraid to talk about it.

I am a Canadian Assistant, Eh!

I live in Ottawa, our nation's capital. I don't live in an igloo or take a dogsled to work and I don't ski in July. I live about *10 clicks* from work and take an OC Transpo bus to get there. Up here OC stands for the County of Ottawa-Carleton, not Orange County.

The first thing most people do in the morning is get a *double-double* coffee and donut at Tim Horton's, or more affectionately known as *Timmy's*. We can pay for it with a *Twoonie* or two *Loonies*. Our troops in Afghanistan have a Timmy's on their base to make them feel at home.

I am doubly blessed with not only having a Canadian accent *eh*, but I also have an Ottawa Valley twang. At work however I am a professional and don't answer the phones with *G'day* or say *see ya* when I say goodbye.

I try to keep my desk *organized* and *co-ordinate* my boss's day. Sometimes my boss can cause a big *kerfuffle* with stressful deadlines and we all go running to *get 'er done*.

I write Canadian English and when I type the letter *z*, I pronounce it *zed*. I requisition *cheques* when I need to pay an invoice and I spell labor -- *L A B O U R*. I try to keep myself professional and younger looking by *colouring* my hair when the *grey* starts showing.

If I go to a restaurant for breakfast I have a choice between white or *brown* toast and when I am finished eating I ask for the *bill*. I go to the *washroom* when nature calls and when I take time off work I say I am on *vacation*. I celebrate Thanksgiving Day on the second Monday in October, not November.

I go out for lunch with the girls at the office and I work across the street from the *lads* on Parliament Hill, where we have a Prime Minister, not a President. Because I work so close to the *Hill*, I have a front row seat to see and hear all the protesters when they come visitin'. Hey, one time the farmers all drove to town and parked their tractors out front and honked their horns all at the same time. Now, that got the politicians' attention eh! When the boys from the Valley come callin', well all I can say is, "We sure know how to *giv'er* up here."

I will still be watching hockey in June and wondering when a Canadian team will win the Stanley Cup and bring it home to Canada where it belongs.

I am looking forward to celebrating Canada Day on July 1st, not July 4th.

Yes, I AM A CANADIAN ASSISTANT eh!

Laughter is the Best Medicine

I love to laugh and to make people laugh. Laughter can get you through many of life's difficult situations and it can be a great stress reliever. A tense situation at work can arise then someone cracks a joke and we laugh. The situation is still there, but now the tension is gone and we have a smile on our face as we try to tackle the problem.

Life is humorous. You can find humour on the bus, at the office and with your family and friends. The funniest things are the things people do and say.

When was the last time you had a real belly laugh? Try to find something to make you laugh. Laugh so hard that your stomach hurts. Laugh so hard that tears are coming out of your eyes. Laughter is good for your soul. We need it every day to keep healthy physically and emotionally.

So have a good laugh whether at work or at home. Better yet, spread a good laugh around. Did you ever notice that laughter is contagious? One person laughs and the next person will start smiling until everyone has been touched by the laughter.